NATION MAKING

EXODUS, NUMBERS, JOSHUA, JUDGES

D1492790

BIBLE GUIDES

The twenty-two volumes

The first eight published volumes are:
1. THE MAKING OF THE BIBLE (*William Barclay*), 13. THE GOOD NEWS (*C. L. Mitton*), 11. THE WISDOM OF ISRAEL (*John Paterson*), 7. PROPHETS OF ISRAEL (1) ISAIAH (*George Knight*), 17. PAUL AND HIS CONVERTS (*F. F. Bruce*), 4. NATION MAKING (*Lawrence E. Toombs*), 5. HISTORIANS OF ISRAEL (1) (*Gordon Robinson*), 6. HISTORIANS OF ISRAEL (2) (*Hugh Anderson*).

BIBLE GUIDES

General Editors: William Barclay and F. F. Bruce

No. 4

NATION MAKING

EXODUS, NUMBERS, JOSHUA, JUDGES

by

LAWRENCE E. TOOMBS

Professor of Old Testament, Drew University,
Madison, N.J., U.S.A.

Published jointly by

LUTTERWORTH PRESS   ABINGDON PRESS
LONDON   NEW YORK AND NASHVILLE

First published 1962

The Biblical quotations in this book are from
the Revised Standard Version of the Bible.

Printed in Great Britain by
Cox & Wyman Ltd., London, Fakenham and Reading

GENERAL INTRODUCTION

THE AIM of Bible Guides is to present in 22 volumes a total view of the Bible, and to present the purpose, plan and power of the Scriptures.

Bible Guides are free from the technicalities of Biblical scholarship but are soundly based on all the generally accepted conclusions of modern Bible research.

They are written in clear, simple, straightforward English. Each author has worked to a comprehensive editorial pattern so that the 22 volumes form a concise conspectus of the Bible.

THE AIM

The aim of Bible Guides is to offer a "guide" to the main themes of each book (or group of books) rather than a commentary on the text of the book. Through Bible Guides the Bible itself will speak its message, reveal its power and declare its purpose.

Bible Guides is essentially an undertaking for non-theologically equipped readers who want to know what the Bible is about, how its various parts came to be written and what their meaning is to-day. But the preacher, teacher, educator and expositor of all ranges of the Christian Church will find Bible Guides a series of books to buy and study. They combine the modern knowledge of the Bible together with all the evangelical zeal of sound Biblical expression—and all done in a handy readable compass.

EDITORIAL PLAN

In our suggestions to the writers of the various books we were careful to make the distinction between a "commentary" and a "guide". Our experience is that an adequate commentary on a book of the Bible requires adequate space and on the part of the student some equipment in the scholarly lore and technicalities of Biblical research. A "guide", however, can be both selective and compressed and do what it sets out to do—guide the reader in an understanding of the book. That has been, and is, our aim.

As general editors we have had a good deal of experience among the various schools of Biblical interpretation. We are constantly surprised at the amount of common Biblical understanding which is acceptable to all types of Christian tradition and churchmanship. We hope that our Bible Guides reflect this and that they will be widely used, and welcomed as a contribution to Biblical knowledge and interpretation in the twentieth century.

THE WRITERS

The writers of Bible Guides represent a widely selected area of Biblical scholars, and all of them have co-operated enthusiastically in the editorial plan. They conceive their work to be that of examination, explanation and exposition of the book(s) of the Bible each is writing about. While they have worked loyally to the pattern we suggested they have been completely free in their presentation. Above all, they have remembered the present power and appeal of the Bible, and have tried to present its message and its authority for life to-day. In this sense Bible Guides is, we think, a fresh venture in the popular understanding of the Scriptures, combined as it is with the scholarly skill of our company of writers. We owe our thanks also to our publishers and their editors, Dr. Emory Stevens Bucke of the Abingdon Press of New York and Nashville, and Dr. Cecil Northcott of the Lutterworth Press of London. Their careful management and attention to publishing detail have given these Bible Guides a world-wide constituency.

WILLIAM BARCLAY

F. F. BRUCE

CONTENTS

THE BANNER OF THE EXODUS

The purpose of this book is to describe the exodus event as it appeared to the Hebrew historians themselves. The sources for such a study should properly include the entire Pentateuch (the first five books of the Old Testament) together with Joshua and Judges and all the references in the prophets and psalmists to the beginnings of Israel's history. The scope of the book is, however, narrower than this. It includes only what might be called the formal and official version of the events recorded in the books of Exodus, Numbers, Joshua and Judges. Genesis, although it is placed before Exodus in our Bibles, is theologically subsequent to the exodus event. That is, it is a meditation on the pre-history of Israel written from the point of view of the community which had experienced the exodus and composed in the light of those events. Leviticus may properly be omitted from our consideration, since it consists entirely of priestly laws and its presence interrupts the flow of the narrative with which we are here principally concerned. The book of Deuteronomy is a profound theology and philosophy of the exodus, so distinctive and penetrating in its analysis of the meaning of the events as to merit treatment in a separate volume.

With the settlement [in Canaan] the drama of the exodus is played out. The decision taken by God in Egypt has reached its fulfilment. The nation has been delivered, consolidated, organized, and provided with a home. The first phase of its history is over. Everything which now happens in Israel and to Israel is interpreted and judged by the events in which the nation was shaped and moulded. The exodus, using the word in the broad sense to include the whole complex of events from the Egyptian bondage to the settlement in Canaan, is formative in the most thorough-going way. Israel is the people whom God brought "out of Egypt, from the house of bondage" (Exodus 13 : 14) and to whom He gave a good land and large, "a land flowing with milk and honey" (13 : 5). She can never escape that fact, never evade its implications, never define herself in any other way, never understand herself in any other terms. She lives from then on under the banner of the exodus. Kings, priests, sages, and prophets must conform their offices to the structure of the covenant. With the exodus event a radically new and transforming power has entered history, which in the course of the centuries will issue in Rabbinic Judaism, in Islam, and in Christianity.

Historically the Israelite nation is the stem of a tree with three main branches. Judaism, retaining the emphasis on the racial and national character of Old Testament religion, concentrated on the terms of the covenant, and, by developing them intensively, became the religion of the Law. Christianity, virtually ignoring the covenant Law, went back to the gracious act of God in liberating the people from bondage, and saw this act renewed, fulfilled, and supplanted in Jesus Christ. It thus became the religion of grace. Islam, elevating the sovereignty of God and the completeness of His control over history, became the religion of submission.

However much their doctrines diverge, all three world religions which hold to belief in one God ultimately stem from the historical experiences of Israel. The making of the nation has had greater consequences for human history than any other single event, and its continuing influence is one of the major forces shaping the future of mankind.

LAWRENCE E. TOOMBS

KEY TO THE NATION

THE BEGINNING of an institution holds special fascination for the people who cherish it in their society. Britons look back with pride to the day in 1215 when the barons forced from King John the guarantees of liberty contained in the Great Charter. In a similar way Americans regard the signing of the Constitution as an event apart from the run-of-the-mill happenings of their history. In both cases the single event is momentous, because it expresses the genius and the spirit of the nation, and provides a key to the rest of its history.

Even after the passage of centuries the people of these nations find themselves personally and emotionally involved with the events. The great documents were signed in their name, and each time the Parliament or the houses of Congress convene they meet under the shadow of the events. Although originating in the past, the signing of the Constitution and the drawing up of the Magna Carta belong equally to the present. The two nations understand themselves in terms of these events. They are the communities of those who share the memory of them. Because they are always present in the memory of the group they still have the power of forming opinion and shaping action centuries after they took place. An event of this quality may be called "a formative event".

Israel's Formative Event

Every human group has its own peculiar formative events. But to no society were these more important than to ancient Israel. Wherever a reader may begin in the Old Testament he sooner or later is brought face to face with the exodus. It forms the subject matter of the first five books of the Bible, and provides the philosophy of history which underlies all of Israel's historical writing. It is the groundwork of the piety of the psalmists, and to the basic tenets of the exodus faith the prophets repeatedly called upon the people to return. In the events of the exodus the political framework of the nation was established, its economic and social ideals settled, and its theology defined. History provides many examples of formative events, but it offers no parallel to the absolute centrality and crucial importance of the exodus in Israel's life and thought.

The exodus not only formed Israel; it changed the face of human history. To gain an impression of the revolutionary quality of Israel's exodus faith one has only to compare it with the religion of the pagan nations which surrounded her. They too had their formative events. The myths in which these events were enshrined were told and retold in the homes of the people and dramatized with pomp and ceremony at the great public religious festivals. In them the pagan community expressed its understanding of the nature of reality and the meaning of life, and through them it sought the power to live life well.

The myths related the deeds of the gods in the "heavenly places" in a timeless realm before the earth and its human population had been created. In this land beyond human experience the dragon of chaos had been defeated, the unruly sea had been driven back within its boundaries, and the death and resurrection of the fertility god had been achieved. In brief, all the elements which went into the stability and order of human society were the results of the activity of the gods in their own pre-historical, or better, non-historical, world.

By celebrating these timeless myths in the festivals of their religion the pagan peoples were, according to their view, putting their society in tune with the great rhythms of nature. They were making available to their communities the very power which had created and was maintaining the universe. The ritual and the myth were, accordingly, not trivialities, but matters of intense

12

seriousness. They dealt, not with fairy tales, but with the substance and meaning of reality itself.

The view of nature expressed in the myths was cyclical. They celebrated perpetual recurrence and eternal return. The vegetation god died annually and his death brought the season of drought and barrenness. He revived annually and his return to life brought back the powers of fertility and growth. In such a framework of thought the stream of time and the events of history have no real meaning. They are accidents or incidents. The truly significant elements of life are the cyclical return of seedtime and harvest, day and night, the new moon after the decay of the old, the summer sun after the weakness of winter. The controlling factor in this cyclic reality, the formative event which gave it birth, was in the realm of the gods outside the ebb and flow of history.

The genius of Israel's exodus faith was that it drew down the divine activity from the sky and out of the field, stream, and forest and placed it within the framework of historical events. God's power operated in Egypt, at the Sea of Reeds, in the wilderness of Sinai, and on the borders of Canaan at a datable time and in the setting of Egyptian culture and nomadic tribal life. Moreover, these formative events were not the result of the interaction of many gods. They occurred because of the deliberate purpose of one deity only, the Lord, who by and through these events became the God of Israel.

God's Crucial Act

By placing the crucial act of God firmly within history, Israelite thought simultaneously broke the cyclic pattern of reality and shattered the polytheism which went hand in hand with it. Since the exodus had happened in history it had consequences in history. The act of God in delivering Israel from Egypt set in motion a chain of events, originating in the mind of God and moving purposefully forward towards a goal decided in advance by God. Process, progress, and movement in history

13

were discerned for the first time by the perceptive eyes of the Hebrew historians.

With this insight a long forward step was taken in man's understanding of himself and his world. Not only were the seeds sown which in their growth produced the three great monotheistic religions of the world, but the foundation was laid for the dynamic view of reality which is a necessary pre-supposition of the whole of western civilization. In addition, nature was robbed of its divinity and represented only as the creation of God and the instrument of His purpose, and the basic concern of God was seen as focused on persons rather than on natural processes. At a single step, therefore, the possibility of an objective view of nature (the basic assumption of science) and the sanctity and value of human personality (the fundamental premise of democratic government) were achieved, although the full development of both was attained only by centuries of struggle and is yet not fully realized.

As it Appeared to the Hebrew Historians

The purpose of this book is to describe the exodus event as it appeared to the Hebrew historians themselves. The sources for such a study should properly include the entire Pentateuch (the first five books of the Old Testament) together with Joshua and Judges and all the references in the prophets and psalmists to the beginnings of Israel's history. The scope of the book is, however, narrower than this. It includes only what might be called the formal and official version of the events recorded in the books of Exodus, Numbers, Joshua and Judges. Genesis, al-though it is placed before Exodus in our Bibles, is theologically subsequent to the exodus event. That is, it is a meditation on the pre-history of Israel written from the point of view of the com-munity which had experienced the exodus and composed in the light of those events. Leviticus may properly be omitted from our consideration, since it consists entirely of priestly laws and its presence interrupts the flow of the narrative with which we are here principally concerned. The book of Deuteronomy is a profound theology and philosophy of the exodus, so distinctive and penetrating in its analysis of the meaning of the events as to merit treatment in a separate volume.

These restrictions leave us with the basic narrative of the making of Israel as our main concern. The story, told with a wealth of detail and a fine sense of drama, resolves itself into eight major elements.

1. The first brief but necessary component of the story is *the slavery of the Israelites in Egypt.* Although it occupies only a relatively few verses (Exodus, chapter 1) it is indispensable to the understanding of the events as a whole. In her best moments Israel realized that when she had been broken and helpless, without merit or strength in herself, God out of His love and grace had performed for her an act of deliverance which she neither deserved nor was able to accomplish for herself. The fact that the nation Israel was born in slavery meant that the God of Israel was above all things a God of deliverance.

2. The second element of the narrative is *the call of Moses* (chapters 2–7: 13) and the revelation to him of the intention of God to rescue Israel from Egypt. In the experience of Moses at the burning bush the exodus is interpreted for the reader *in advance* so that it is impossible for him to see it in any other light than as an act of God.

3. *The deliverance itself* is then described (chapters 7: 14–18). In this section miracle is piled on miracle. The devastating plagues in Egypt culminating in the destruction of the first-born of men and animals, exempting not even the house of the Pharaoh, is succeeded by the miraculous crossing of the Sea of Reeds and the overthrow of the pursuing Egyptian charioteers. The apparent disregard for factual accuracy in these stories is sometimes offensive to the modern reader, schooled to think in terms of the inviolable laws of nature. In the narrative they have one purpose only—to underline with all possible vigour the conviction that at every stage in the deliverance the power of God, not that of Israel, is the operative and creative force.

4. The fourth element in the exodus is *the giving of the covenant at Sinai* (chapters 19–40). In this experience the nation was made. Its political structure, and its ethical and legal ideals, were given in outline, later to be hugely elaborated by successive generations of Israelite leadership. However, the political and legal aspects are, strictly speaking, side issues or derivative elements of the covenant. The relationship established at Sinai between the people and its God is the determinative and all-important aspect of the formation of the covenant.

5. Interwoven with the story of the Sinai Covenant and continuing on into the later narrative is the motif of *the murmuring and complaint of the people against God*. The most familiar graphic illustrations of infant Israel's rebellious tendency are the episode of the Golden Calf and the refusal of the people to march directly into Canaan. However, the "murmuring tradition" is so often repeated in so many different forms that it must be considered a major emphasis of the narrative. The tension between the delivering God and His faithless people is thus present in the story of Israel's formative beginning, providing an historical basis for the later prophetic denunciations of apostasy and immorality.

6. The motif of *the forty years' wandering of Israel* in the wilderness is not really distinct from the "murmuring tradition". The faint-heartedness of Israel condemned her to wait in the desert until time and death had disposed of the generation which refused to risk an immediate invasion of Canaan. Nevertheless, the events of the forty years are important enough to be treated separately.

7. In the accounts of *the taking of the land of Canaan* the ups and downs of history, its mixture of successes and failures, tend to be swallowed up in the concept of a triumphant march of the people of God under the divine guidance into a homeland from which the divine leader miraculously clears the pagan inhabitants (Joshua 1–12, and Judges 2 : 1–5). It is clear, however, that in the minds of the Hebrew writers the taking of the land was the goal to which the process of divine deliverance, begun in Egypt, moved.

8. The exodus event ends with *the division of the land* and *the settlement of the tribes* according to a system decreed by the God of Israel.

With the settlement the drama of the exodus is played out. The decision taken by God in Egypt has reached its fulfilment. The nation has been delivered, consolidated, organized, and provided with a home. The first phase of its history is over. Everything which now happens in Israel and to Israel is interpreted and judged by the events in which the nation was shaped and moulded. The exodus, using the word in the broad sense to include the whole complex of events from the Egyptian bondage to the settlement in Canaan, is formative in the most thorough-going way. Israel is the people whom God brought "out of Egypt, from the house of bondage" (Exodus 13: 14) and to whom He gave a good land and large, "a land flowing with milk and honey" (13: 5). She can never escape that fact, never evade its implications, never define herself in any other way, never understand herself in any other terms. She lives from then on under the banner of the exodus. Kings, priests, sages, and prophets must conform their offices to the structure of the covenant. With the exodus event a radically new and transforming power has entered history, which in the course of the centuries will issue in Rabbinic Judaism, in Islam, and in Christianity.

Structure of the Story

It is instructive to compare the eight major themes, isolated and described above, with the four which Dr. Martin Noth has determined on the basis of his form-critical method. By a study of literary form and structure Noth separates out as independent elements of Israelite tradition: the exodus from Egypt, the entrance into the land of Canaan, the wandering in the wilderness, and the revelation at Sinai. His fifth theme, the promise to the patriarchs, lies outside the sphere of this book. In Noth's view of the history of Israelite tradition these elements had an independent origin, and existed as separate units for some considerable time before being brought together in a firm narrative pattern beginning with the Egyptian bondage and ending with the settlement. Even if Noth's analysis is not accepted in all its details, it is evident that the present form of the exodus story is the complex end result of the weaving together of a great many originally distinct stories.

How did it come about that these diverse traditions were welded into a unity? We have seen how the pagan religions made use of the myths in their worship, dramatizing them in the public festivals. Israel's new formative beginning displaced the myths from their position in the ritual. No longer could they use the myth of creation or of the dying and rising God to express their view of the essential nature of reality. In keeping with their new historical beginning, the Israelites celebrated an annual covenant renewal ceremony, and in this festival the place of the myth was taken by the recital of the series of mighty acts by which God had called the nation into existence. In the context of the covenant ceremony the official form of the exodus narrative took shape. The tribes in solemn assembly recited their history in such a way as to emphasize what God had done in their behalf, and renewed their declaration of allegiance to Him. These recitations of the saving act of God became the crystallizing centres around which other traditions from a variety of sources were gathered to amplify and strengthen the simple outline of the story.

Ritual Recitation of the Story

The community recitation of the exodus event was so important in shaping the thought of the Old Testament that Dr. G. Ernest Wright defines Biblical theology as a whole as "the confessional recital of the redemptive acts of God" (*God Who Acts*, p. 13). A reflection of this ancient phenomenon can be seen in the Sacrament of the Lord's Supper when the words of the institution are recited as an integral part of the ritual. A modification of the Israelite covenant renewal ceremony is preserved in the Methodist order for a covenant service usually celebrated at the New Year.

The oldest and briefest statements of the exodus event, suitable for recitation in worship, are to be found in Deuteronomy 6: 20–25 and 26: 5–9. The first of these is given as the formula by which a parent is to answer the child who wants to know the meaning of the national religion. It emphasizes the Egyptian slavery, the miraculous quality of the deliverance, God's gift of the land to His people, and the giving of the Law to the nation. All is represented as the doing of God rather than of Israel, and although the father and son may be talking together generations after the actual events, they think of themselves as having been present and having experienced the deliverance. The father says, "*We* were Pharaoh's slaves in Egypt; and the Lord brought *us* out of Egypt with a mighty hand." The second passage belongs even more clearly to the setting of worship. It is the ritual for the presentation of First Fruits. After bringing his offering to the priest the worshipper declares his faith in words which amount to a little summary of the exodus event. It contains the same elements as the first passage with the addition of a statement referring briefly to Jacob, "A wandering Aramean was my father". The worshipper's sense of his own involvement in the events which he recites is again clear. He speaks of the deliverance from oppression in Egypt as something which happened to him.

A longer ritual confession of the exodus faith appears in Joshua 24: 2–13. The section dealing with Abraham, Isaac, and Jacob is much expanded, and this is followed by a detailed recital of the deliverance, the wilderness wanderings, and the conquest of Canaan, described as deeds of God. Although in its present setting this confession forms the prelude to the covenant made between God and Israel at Shechem under the leadership of Joshua, its form gives us a clear indication of how the ancient Israelites were accustomed to confess their basic faith at the public gatherings of the tribes.

To summarize, very soon after the exodus took place the

tribes were celebrating an annual festival of remembrance and renewal, centred probably at the city of Shechem. The ritual of this and similar festivals established the official order and form in which the events ought to be told. It established also an emphasis, never to be lost, on the initiative and activity of God in the events, and on the participation in them of all succeeding generations of Israelites.

The Basis of Israel's Unity

Something like this had to be done in order to preserve the unity of the Israelite tribes during the troubled and uncertain first two centuries of their occupation of Canaan. They were not a natural unity. The people who left Egypt were, as the Bible says, "a mixed multitude" (Exodus 12: 38) consisting of the deposit of many centuries of Semitic infiltration into Egypt. In this group there must have been a nucleus of people who remembered the traditions of Abraham, Isaac, and Jacob and regarded Palestine as their native land. But there were also many others who were drawn to Moses simply because they were Semites and slaves. So disorganized and varied were the fugitives from Egypt that they had no tribal or other authority and depended on the personal leadership of Moses alone until, guided by his father-in-law, Jethro (a Midianite), Moses gave them an organization of a military type by dividing them into thousands, hundreds, fifties, and tens (Exodus 18). This diverse group left Egypt about 1290 B.C. They remained in the wilderness for forty years, perfecting their organization and developing their hardihood and fighting qualities. Along the line of march in the wilderness they picked up and added to their number other more or less closely related nomadic groups. About 1250 B.C., now a formidable fighting force, they struck at the Canaanite cities in Palestine.

The first to fall was Jericho, the strongly fortified city which guarded the eastern approaches to the land. The weight of the Israelite power then fell on the cities in the south of the country,

and Lachish, Bethel, Debir, and Shiloh were destroyed. Archae-
ology dramatically confirms the capture of these cities about 1250
B.C. No mention is made, however, of the taking of Shechem.
Yet this is the city at which the tribes assembled to hear the fare-
well speech of the aged commander, Joshua (see Joshua 24). The
case of Shechem indicates that whole areas of the country,
particularly in the central highlands, fell into Israelite hands
without a struggle. Almost certainly, then, these localities were
already in the hands of peoples sympathetic to the invaders.

The Amarna letters, Egyptian royal documents dating from
1400 to 1350 B.C., indicate that two centuries before the exodus
a Semitic people called the Hapiru (compare Hebrew) was
gradually infiltrating into Palestine and taking over the control
of a number of cities there. One of these was Shechem. The
people who had entered the land in 1400 B.C. and thereafter
almost certainly joined hands with the fugitives from Egypt,
entered into covenant with them and adopted their exodus
tradition. Out of tribal groups with varied origins there was
thus formed a twelve-tribe league, dedicated to the worship of
the God who had revealed Himself to Moses, sharing the tradition of the exodus experiences, and pledged to make common
cause in time of war. Because of their diversified origin, and
because of the pressures towards paganism to which the environment of Canaan continuously exposed them, the tribes needed
to be constantly reminded of the basis of their unity and to be
recalled to the covenant on which their existence as a distinctive
people rested.

Historical and theological forces united to produce the confessional recitals of the exodus faith, and these in turn became the
basis of the expansion of the short creeds into the long and detailed story of the exodus which now appears in our Bible. The
first decisive step in the formation of the longer narrative
probably took place about 950 B.C., in the reign of Solomon,
when an unknown author in the southern half of the country
composed a large-scale history of the making of Israel. The
writer, known by the symbol J, fleshed out the bare outline of

the earlier creeds with a complex of traditions drawn from the shrines and sacred places of the land, shaping them into a coherent, vivid, and theologically powerful interpretation of the events. A century or so later (about 850 B.C.) another writer, known as E, performed the same service for the northern part of the country. These two documents, closely parallel in their order and content, were combined into a single narrative about 700 B.C. The last stage in the development of the exodus story is the addition to the combined J and E narrative of a large body of additional material drawn from a priestly history of Israel, and hence called P. The J and E narrative, supplemented by P, was in final form by 400 B.C. and is the exodus story with which Bible readers are familiar.

The literary condition in Joshua and Judges is somewhat different and will be treated in the next chapter.

2

SOURCES OF THE STORY

A GLANCE at the hymn book of any Christian denomination shows sacred songs from a wide variety of sources. Latin hymns stand next to Biblical psalms and gospel songs. The book is saved from confusion only by the careful way in which the editors have numbered all the selections, and listed the names of authors and composers with appropriate dates. Even with the benefit of this editorial work an observer from another planet might be surprised to hear a man in a twentieth-century suit with a twentieth-century mind singing lustily, and with no sense of incongruity, "Were all the world with devils filled". The last thing the man would expect to see in his suburban world would be a demon, but he retains the tradition of them and their baleful influences from his religious past and they have symbolic meaning for him.

The books of the Old Testament have somewhat the same quality as the hymn book. They are a compilation of traditions from various sources. They lack, however, the conscientious separation of one tradition from another, and they never preserve authors' names and dates. Moreover, many primitive traditions, like the demons in modern worship, were preserved, although their original meaning was much altered by the passage of time.

The unravelling of the sources of the Biblical writings has occupied the attention of scholars since the principles of literary criticism were first applied to the Bible. Twenty-five years ago students were referring to the "assured results" of this study. The certainty has pretty much evaporated. All that is universally agreed is that the Biblical books are compilations of material from various sources.

The Four Source-Documents

The first five books of the Old Testament are a case in point. When Biblical scholars were talking of "assured results" it was generally accepted that Genesis, Exodus, Leviticus, Numbers, and Deuteronomy had four main sources. These were extensive historical works, called by the letters J, E, D, and P. The four documents had been edited and drawn together into a single work, but the seams of the joining still showed, and a sharp-eyed analyst could separate the four strands.

Of course, the four documents were not the beginning of Israelite tradition. Long before they were written the stories and poems, laws and legends, which went into their make-up, had been memorized, and passed on from generation to generation by word of mouth. The fantastic memories of unlettered primitive people is a well-known fact, and the literature need not have suffered much distortion before it was committed to writing.

J and the Creation

The document J, composed probably during or just after the reign of Solomon, begins with the creation of the world, and continues with a series of rather disconnected stories about the ages just before and after the flood. J's style is racy and picturesque. He has a naïve view of God, picturing Him as a big man with all the passions and limitations of human nature. He uses the personal name of Israel's God, the Lord, from the beginning. In spite of the picturesque and sometimes primitive quality of his work, J is a profound thinker, and he uses his stories skilfully to show the nature of man and his need for redemption. He then passes to the narrative of the Patriarchs, Abraham, Isaac, and Jacob, where he is mainly interested in God's promise that He will form a nation from the descendants of Abraham. When we pick up J at the beginning of the book of Exodus, he is dealing with the Egyptian enslavement of Israel, and we will follow him from this point to the entrance to the promised land.

E—A Lofty View of God

E has a loftier view of God than J, and a less vigorous style. Dreams and angels are common in his writing as ways in which God communicates with men. He does not use "the Lord" until after the revelation to Moses. He starts his history with the Patriarchs and goes on to the entrance into Canaan closely parallel to J.

In the final edition of the sections of the Old Testament which we are studying J and E were woven closely together, and for our purposes they may be treated as a unit. Readers who would like to see how the division may be worked out may consult W. O. E. Oesterley and T. H. Robinson, *An Introduction to the Books of the Old Testament*, or any other standard Old Testament introduction.

The Character of D and P

P is quite different from J and E. It is written in a stilted style, and displays a depressing interest in dates, genealogies, and lists of cities. The God of P is even more lofty and remote than that of E, and His personal name is not revealed until the time of Moses. The document is interested in the priests, the sacrifice, and the ritual, and for that reason is called the priestly document. Although it is late in origin (about 400 B.C.), it contains much early and valuable tradition.

D is a harder literary unit to handle, because there is much dispute about its limits. It certainly begins with the book of Deuteronomy, and the position adopted here is that it is directly continued by Joshua, Judges, Samuel, and Kings. This view is not universally held, and many believe that Joshua should be analysed into the documents J, E, and P.

In this book we are taking the following position. In Exodus and Numbers a rough breakdown into the composite document JE will be recognized, but no finer distinctions will be made. Material from this source will be treated before the priestly material. As for Joshua and Judges, they will be dealt with as a unit, taken from the middle of the Deuteronomic history, which began with Deuteronomy itself and was continued by Samuel and Kings.

An additional word about the book of Joshua is in order. Its authors were probably Levites, members of the priestly group in Israel. Their writing, therefore, resembles the P document in interest and outlook. But the Levites were also teachers of the law, and because of this office they were deeply sympathetic to the Sinai tradition. The latter fact gives their books a prophetic as well as a priestly accent.

Origins—A Specialized Study

A minimum of critical analysis appears in this book. The reason is twofold. In the first place the uncertainty among experts as to the proper literary analysis urges caution. Secondly, in a book of this size excessive dealing with sources would divert attention from the main aim, which is to explain the message of the Biblical books as they now stand.

It is hoped that the reader will not attribute this neglect to lack of interest in literary questions. The story of how the oral tradition, preserved in the sacred places in ancient Israel, was gathered around the structure of the covenant creeds, and fashioned into a running history of the nation, is a fascinating one. Old songs, riddles, little collections of laws, hero stories and legends were all drawn into the narrative and made to express the faith that was in the nation. It would be unkind and unjust to neglect the work of generations of authors and thinkers who laboured to form the literary masterpiece of the exodus story. The reader whose interest is aroused by these pages will find it a most valuable next stage to investigate these matters further.

A final word should be said in explanation of the system of

references used in the following four chapters. Since the volume is designed as a guide to the reading of the Scriptures, it is liberally sprinkled with references. Some of these are only incidental and illustrative. In other cases what is being said is based directly on a particular Biblical passage, which is, therefore, indispensable to an understanding of the section. These key passages are pointed out to the reader by the use of the word *"Reference"* before them. It will help a good deal if they are read in conjunction with the text.

3

INTO THE WILDERNESS

THE EXODUS from Egypt (*Reference* Exodus 1–15, basically JE) took place during the 19th Dynasty, when the powerful Ramses II (1290–1224 B.C.) occupied the throne of the oldest kingdom on earth. In Ramses' day Egypt was already hoary with age, and conservatism lay like a disease on her people. The pyramids were antiquities, the inscrutable sphinx had been looking down on the desert for over thirteen centuries, and the arts of government, literature, and architecture had been practiced for so long that they had been reduced to unalterable tradition. Artists continued to distort the human figure into a strange mixture of profile and full-face, and scribes still wrote in the pleasing but cumbersome hieroglyphic system because custom had made these techniques sacred.

The traditionalism of Egypt was not the result of stupidity or lack of imagination. It arose from a fierce national pride. In the Egyptian language the citizens of the Nile Valley were "people"; the rest of the world, "foreigners". The inhabitants of Palestine were scornfully dismissed as "miserable Asiatics". The oldest and best civilization in the world had its reputation to maintain, and it did so by zealous conservation of its past. Three centuries before Ramses' accession the national pride had been rudely jolted. A mixed people with a generous proportion of Semites among them had conquered the northern part of Egypt and put a foreigner in the Pharaoh's seat. During the one hundred and fifty years of their control (about 1750–1600 B.C.) these Hyksos, as the Egyptians called them, diligently aped Egyptian ways, but their efforts brought them no affection from the Egyptians, and when native Egyptians, Amosis I and

Amenophis I, gathered enough strength to drive the miserable Asiatics northward into Palestine and Syria, Egypt rejoiced to see them go.

The Hyksos interlude is important in Biblical history because it was during their régime that the Israelites went down into Egypt. The foreign Pharaohs welcomed Semites and gave them preferential treatment. Thus, the Hebrew, Joseph, could become Prime Minister. When, however, the native Pharaohs regained control this favouritism ended, and resurgent nationalism expressed itself in hatred of the foreigner. The Semitic elements of the population were reduced to slavery and their descendants were building the palaces and public works of Ramses II when Moses came among them with a message of liberty and hope. The actual time lapse between the expulsion of the Hyksos under Amosis I and the reign of Ramses II is 300 years, but the Biblical narrative collapses it into a single eloquent sentence, "There arose a new king over Egypt, who did not know Joseph" (Exodus 1 : 8).

The oppression in Egypt left an indelible impression on the Hebrew mind. *Exodus* portrays the Egyptians as a cruelly self-centred people, caring more for their buildings than for their slaves, with a taint of sadism in their nature, and with a hard-hearted, hard-headed man to rule over them. If the slaughter of the children to hold down the slave population, the denial of straw to the brickmakers apparently for the pleasure of seeing them fall short of their quota, and the too ready use of the lash remind the reader uncomfortably of Nazi policy and practice, he may recall that it was an Old Testament writer who said, "There is nothing new under the sun" (Ecclesiastes 1 : 9). It must be added in fairness that the Biblical account is biased in favour of the Hebrews. A parallel Egyptian record would undoubtedly read differently.

The purpose of the story is not basically to express hatred for the Egyptians but to emphasize the greatness of God's act of deliverance. Intransigent and vicious power was pitted against His will. The opponent had the wisdom of the ages and the wealth of nations on its side. Israel had nothing; neither arms nor organization, strength nor hope. If she was to be delivered, God's power, not her own, must break the yoke of Egypt.

This fact of Israel's historic experiences became a foundation stone of her religion. Since she had started literally from nothing, she owed everything she was and had to her God. Thus Israel learned something decisive about herself and about the God she worshipped. The nation was absolutely dependent on God for every element of her economic, political, and social life. But the God on whom she must rely is the kind of God who directs His unlimited power towards the liberation of the helpless.

This insight is an important key to the understanding of the entire Old Testament, for Biblical religion cannot be understood in terms of self-reliance. The prophets and leaders of Israel were in stark opposition to any confidence in human powers, and their perpetual task was to recall Israel to the fundamental fact of her existence, namely, that without total dependence on God the nation had no past and no future.

The same attitude, stripped of its national emphasis, passed over into Christianity where it is taught that the human being is incapable by his own power of fulfilling any of the deepest needs of his nature. The Christian confesses that he owes his very life to the delivering act of God in Jesus Christ and that he cannot sustain that life except by the power of Christ working in him. St. Paul is in the spirit of the exodus faith when he writes, "What have you that you did not receive?" (1 Corinthians 4: 7.)

Moses, the Leader

These fundamental features of Old Testament religion are further illustrated and amplified in the experience of Moses. (*Reference* Exodus 2: 1–6: 1.)

The story of the slave child set adrift in a boat of rushes to save him from the Egyptian executioners, his rescue by the princess, and his upbringing in the court as a protégé of the king is too well known to need much comment. A similar tale is told in Akkadian literature about the great king, Sargon I. The Biblical writers evidently borrowed a well-known hero motif and adapted it to their purpose of showing how long before the event itself God was preparing the way for the exodus. The story of Moses' infancy is, therefore, a dramatic illustration of the Old Testament principle that in the decisive hours of history it is God who acts.

The youthful Moses early began to display the qualities which made him the superb servant of God and the nation-maker which he later became. His training in statecraft and military strategy, received at court, unquestionably stood him in good stead when he faced the difficult problem of organizing the Israelites and leading them on the march through the wilderness. But they are not the most significant qualities of his nature. He had the rare capacity of sympathy for the sufferings of others and the still rarer willingness to risk his own comfortable future in order to identify himself with them (Exodus 2: 11). He had a fine sense of justice, which qualified him well for his later role as lawgiver. His leading legal principle, that the function of the law is to protect the weak from the oppressive power of the strong, became an essential part of every Old Testament legal code and provided the impetus for the prophetic demand for social justice. Moses himself exemplified the principle in his defense of the Hebrew slave (2: 11) and in the protection he offered to the Midianite girls when they were threatened by a mob of bullying shepherds (2: 15–20). The impetuosity which

31

made him draw his sword against the Egyptian slave master and then flee for his life into the desert, and later caused him to smash the tablets of the law among the rocks at the foot of the Golden Calf (32: 1–35), was a necessary counterbalance to his sensitivity to the needs of the people under his charge and his self-effacing willingness to serve their best interests (Numbers 12). Nations are not made by thinking machines, calculating every move according to the dictates of prudence and self-preservation. It is, perhaps, symbolic that this complex and sensitive man never entered the promised land, but only saw it "from afar". He was of that uncommon breed of men for whom to serve God and the people well is its own reward.

No higher tribute could be paid to Moses than that accorded him by the Biblical writers. They regard him, not only as the national leader, but as the founder of the prophetic, priestly, and legal traditions of Israel.

Moses' Encounter with God

The importance attached to the call of Moses is shown by the fact that each of the major sources has an extended version of this (*Reference* Exodus 3: 1—6: 1, JE; Exodus 6: 1—7: 13, P). Those who dislike the idea of founding religion on "personal experience" sometimes minimize the significance of Moses' encounter with God. They would rather emphasize the objective character of Israel's faith and its origin in God's activity in concrete historical events. Rightly understood, the call of Moses provides no ground for interpreting religion in terms of personal piety and allowing it to become a mere matter of how the individual stands in relation to God. How better could the writers declare that the deliverance from Egypt was not the result of a lucky combination of political circumstances, but the outworking of a deliberate purpose of God, than by showing that God had announced and interpreted His action in advance of the event? What happened to Moses was not for himself, but for Israel and for the future.

The objective element in Moses' call is immediately apparent in the way God identified Himself, "I am the God of your father, the God of Abraham, the God of Isaac, and the God of Jacob" (Exodus 3 : 6). Five centuries after the oath to the Fathers God was about to bring His promise to reality. Such a God cannot be bound by time or history, but must Himself be in control of events, determining the destiny of men and nations. Similarly, since God spoke to Moses in Midian about an action He would perform in Egypt, He must be free of the limitations of space and geography.

A God who Delivers

But to see God as unlimited by time and space may be only to see Him in terms of brute force. Accordingly the sentence in which the motive for God's action is expressed is one of the most significant in the Old Testament. "I have seen the affliction of my people . . . and I have come down to deliver them" (Exodus 3 : 7–8). The God who revealed Himself to Moses was moved to action by human suffering, and, when confronted by injustice and brutality, He took action to liberate the oppressed. Israel's slavery, not her intrinsic worth or nobility, drew God's attention to her and led Him to act in her behalf.

Two consequences follow from this understanding of the motivation of God. First, He is a God of grace, of outgoing love directed towards the weak and helpless, who are the special objects of His care. This means that His characteristic action is that of deliverance. The large place occupied by the concept of salvation in the Judeo-Christian tradition is traceable to the fact that from the beginning the God of that tradition is one who always and everywhere labours to set the people free. The second consequence, no less far reaching in its implications, is that by virtue of her origin Israel could make no claim upon the special regard of God. She was not delivered from Egypt because of meritorious service. She had nothing to recommend her but her scars and no claim upon God except the moral claim which suffering makes upon love. That God chose Israel was the sovereign act of His own free grace, unforced by any righteousness or goodness on the side of the nation.

A Nation Called to Service

These facts about God's choice of Israel (often technically referred to as "election") take a good deal of the sting from the idea of a Chosen People. The concept means neither that Israel was the moral superior of all other races, nor that God was playing favourites in her case. He chose her because of her need, and, as a consequence of her unique response to His act, she became His servant and representative before the world.

Israel's call to service, rather than to special privilege, is splendidly illustrated in a passage from the P document, which, although it comes later in the narrative, may conveniently be treated at this point. "You shall be my own possession among all peoples; for all the earth is mine, and you shall be to me a kingdom of priests and a holy nation" (Exodus 19: 5, 6). Here the world-wide range of God's purpose in the election of Israel is expressed. She is a nation set apart from all others for the special service of God (i.e., she is holy). The nature of this service is that she is to be a priest to the world, her function being to bring the nations before God and God before the nations. By implication Israel is to be the means for the extension to others of the call which she herself has heard and to which she has responded. Accepting this task, the nation accepts not only privileges and advantages, but also hard and demanding responsibilities. Like Jonah faced with the prospect of preaching to Nineveh, Israel would on many occasions in her history gladly have been free of the election, if she could also be rid of its responsibilities.

God's Name

In response to Moses' question God revealed His "name". To the Hebrew mind the "name" is more than a convenient way of referring to a person. It is the symbol and summary of his nature, so that Moses' inquiry as to the name of God is in reality a request to know what God is like.

The personal name of Israel's God is a Hebrew word usually translated "the Lord". The precise meaning of this name is uncertain, and some scholars have seen in it a reference to a God of the storm or of the mountain. The most convincing explanation is that the name is derived from the causative form of the verb "to be", meaning, therefore, "he who causes things to happen". This understanding of the name is most appropriate to the God of the exodus who breaks into history "with a mighty hand and an outstretched arm" (Deuteronomy 7: 19).

The name "the Lord" was not, however, revealed directly to Moses. The form of the verb was changed to that of direct speech, "I am". "Say to the people of Israel, 'I AM has sent me to you'" (Exodus 3: 14). This revelation was directly pointed to the situation confronting Moses. Instead of the generalized conviction that God is one who causes things to happen, the name given to Moses indicated that God was about to bring His creative power into action now in the specific case of the slavery of Israel.

In addition, the indirectness of God's answer to Moses is in keeping with the Old Testament idea that God's nature is not open to the full scrutiny and understanding of men. His revelation is not on demand, even to such an outstanding servant as Moses. He chooses the time, the place, and the nature of the revelation in accordance with His own purpose.

The same point is made in a later story, again revolving around a request of Moses for more knowledge of God (Exodus 33: 17–23, J). Moses asked to see God's glory. This request was refused outright, and Moses was permitted to see only God's back, after He had passed by. He could not predict or control God's coming, but could only see the results of His action after it had passed.

This emphasis on the mystery surrounding the nature of God leads us to consider a feature of the call of Moses which appears at the beginning of the narrative, but which is better understood when the whole experience is before us. The ground on which Moses stood was "holy ground", made holy by the presence there of the holy God (Exodus 3 : 5). The concept of the holiness of God underlies the entire narrative, and, indeed, the whole of the exodus story.

The concept of holiness has exceedingly primitive roots. It refers to the aweful, majestic and deadly power resident in a deity. Holiness is that which separates the human from the divine, and since it is the very essence of divinity, a human being can come in contact with it only at peril of his life. Any object used in worship, or any person set apart for the service of the deity, becomes holy by his close association with the holiness of God, and he must take every ritual precaution to avoid offending against the holy deity. Thus Moses must remove his shoes before he touches the earth made holy by the presence of God. Thus too his face shines so that the people cannot bear to look at it when he comes from the mountain where he has been in close contact with the divine (Exodus 34 : 29–35), and for the same reason the mountain itself is out of bounds to the people encamped at its foot (19 : 10–15).

Out of this primitive concept the Old Testament developed two main emphases. The holiness of God indicates His otherness and difference from man, and this difference consists in the perfection of God in contrast to the sinfulness and weakness of human nature. The miracle of the exodus faith is its conviction that the holy God does not choose to remain remote from men, but to draw near to them in acts of deliverance. The perfection of God expresses itself in His gracious approach to Israel, but His holiness prevents Israel from ever taking Him for granted or attempting to engage Him on terms of equality. The "fear of

God", shown by Moses (Exodus 3 : 6) and often referred to elsewhere in the Old Testament, is not terror, but the due and sober recognition of the holiness of God.

The Priestly document adds little to the call of Moses, except to place the priest, Aaron, at his side as his advisor and spokesman.

A Contest Between Gods
Reference Exodus 7–11

The narrative is now transferred to Egypt and takes on the aspect of a monumental struggle between Moses and Aaron on one side and the magicians and the Pharaoh on the other. The atmosphere of magic which pervades the story is foreign to modern thought. The staff that blossoms or turns into a serpent when thrown on the ground, and the plagues called down by Moses upon Egypt (the first two of which were duplicated by the Egyptian magicians) belong to a world before the birth of science. The mind of this early age, possessing no concept of natural law, is not disturbed by apparent violations of the natural order. In fact, it looks for them as evidences that the divine powers are at work, and, when it finds them, it inflates them in order to increase the wonder, and to ensure that the reader will be aware of the presence and activity of God in the events.

The disasters in Egypt during the preaching of Moses have in this way been systematized into a scheme of ten plagues, the final edition combining J, E, and P sources. These are the turning of water into blood and the plagues of frogs, gnats, flies, cattle disease, boils, hail, locusts, darkness, and the death of the firstborn. The composite list is represented as ten successive stages of a contest between the God of Israel and the Pharaoh. This is nothing less than a struggle between gods, for according to Egyptian theology the ruler of Egypt was the incarnation of the god Horus, the Lord of Heaven. The servants of Pharaoh-Horus pit themselves against the servants of the Lord. After the second contest they fail, but the Pharaoh will not acknowledge his defeat until the scourge of death claims his son. On his own home ground the god of Egypt is no match for the God of Israel, and, although he can delay the fulfilment of God's purpose, his action only brings suffering on his people and in the end comes to nothing.

The climax of the plagues is the passing of the angel of death (a standard Hebrew expression for plague) through the land of Egypt, and the death of the firstborn. The Israelites, forewarned of the disaster and under the protection of the Lord, did not suffer the death of their children. While the angel of death was passing they ate their last meal in Egypt with "their loins girded, their sandals on their feet, and their staff in their hand" (Exodus 12: 11, P), ready for a hasty departure from the land of slavery.

The Passover

The Passover, commemorative of this event, became the most important annual religious festival of Israel. It was an essential part of the fabric of the nation, serving as a perpetual reminder of the formative events from which the nation came. The J writer puts it succinctly, "When your children say to you, 'What do you mean by this service?' you shall say, 'It is the sacrifice of the Lord's passover, for he passed over the houses of the people of Israel in Egypt, when he slew the Egyptians but spared our houses'" (Exodus 12: 26–27).

Although the Passover was originally a festival held by the nomads at the time of the calving of the flocks, it was adopted by the Israelites and baptized into their distinctive exodus faith. It is quite probable that Exodus 1–15 was read annually at the celebration of the Passover, and that this community repetition gave the story the form in which it has come down to us.

What has been said of the Passover is true of the other prominent festivals of ancient Israel, the feast of Harvest or Weeks and the feast of Ingathering or Tabernacles (Exodus 23: 14–17). These are pre-Israelite in origin and were obviously based on the agricultural year, but under the magic of the exodus faith they became memorials of the deliverance from Egypt.

Israelite worship as seen in the festivals is a community expression of gratitude for the saving act of God, a public identification of the present generation with the nation established by that act, a communal confession of sin against the God of deliverance, and a common prayer for the presence in the existing community of the saving power of the God who brought it into being. This concept of worship had no small part in the making of the nation, and its leading ideas have passed over into Christianity, where the Church relates itself in a very similar way to the saving act of God in Jesus Christ.

4

SUMMONED TO SINAI

THE CALL of Moses, the defeat of the Egyptians' magicians, the plagues in Egypt, and the institution of the Passover have set the scene for great events to follow. The Israelites have been introduced to their God and have seen the impact of His power on the strongest nation on earth. But the climax of the drama is not yet reached. The "mixed multitude" will only become a nation when it is brought to the holy mountain, Mt. Sinai (called Mt. Horeb in E), and confronted with the demands of God in the form of the Law. Before proceeding to this crucial event, however, the writers give one last dramatic illustration of the total dependence of the people on the God who brought them into the wilderness; the deliverance at the Sea of Reeds.

Deliverance at the Sea

The Israelites left Egypt, not by the easy coastal road, but in a south-easterly direction into the marshy country between the Gulf of Suez and the Mediterranean. Here they came to a place called in Hebrew the Sea of Reeds. The traditional identification of the spot with the Red Sea is a persistent error of interpretation. The Egyptian charioteers of the border guard were in hot pursuit, and the Israelites found themselves in a hopeless position between the marshes and the enemy. In the moment of despair when they were alternately calling on God and cursing Moses an east wind, hot and dry from the desert, made the surface of the marsh hard enough to carry the lightly-equipped Israelites. The pursuing chariots bogged down on the treacherous surface, and the pursuit came to a sudden end.

Israelite tradition was not prepared to dismiss this event as a lucky accident of wind and weather, or even as a proof of the aphorism that "fortune favours the brave". Rather it was to them the supreme example of God's intervention in history on behalf of his people. As time passed the story gathered more and more miraculous elements. According to E, Moses struck the waters with his marvelous rod and they divided (Exodus 14: 16). In the P narrative the water stood up on either side and the Israelites passed through a sunken roadway between walls of immobilized water (14: 22).

The modern mind is likely to regard this as superstitious miracle making, but to the Biblical authors the physical details were secondary to the meaning of the story. The writers wished to make it absolutely clear that the Israelites did not win through to freedom by their courage or prowess. In the hour of their helplessness liberty was given to them by the action of God.

God or Chance?

Appreciation of this point allows the reader to understand many other features in the narrative. The pillar of fire and the pillar of cloud which guided the marching Israelites and showed them where to pitch camp (Exodus 13: 21), the quails (Numbers 11: 31–35), manna (Exodus 16: 1–36), and water from the rock (Numbers 20: 1–13) by which they were nourished in a desert where there was little or no sustenance for the traveller, are all symbols pointing to the same reality. This was no ordinary migration of tribes from one home to another. The route was chosen by God, food and water were provided by Him, and He won the victories.

A great deal of ingenuity has been displayed in showing how flights of quails could have appeared in the desert at exactly the right moment, on how manna is really the sweet, sticky sap of a desert plant, and on how water can be struck from a rock by anyone fortunate enough to hit upon the source of an underground spring. Even if all the marvelous happenings in the wilderness could be explained as perfectly natural the basic question would remain unanswered, "Was it God or chance?" In the vivid, pictorial language characteristic of Hebrew literature the writers insist that at every point in the escape from Egypt God was active. The experience taught them, and they taught their children, that the God of Israel was a liberating God, a God who provided sustenance, guidance, and protection for His people, and that ultimately the survival of the nation depended on its living by the fact that without its God it was nothing and could do nothing.

The real questions raised by the exodus narrative are not those of the factual accuracy of what is told. The story is not true because its physical details can be demonstrated or false if they prove to be inaccurate. It is true only if its insight into the nature of God and into the character and need of man is valid. Is God in truth a God who leads, upholds and provides for the needs of His people? Is the human being incapable of working out his own deliverance? These are questions of permanent significance which the exodus raises, and its truth must be judged in the light of its answers to them.

This interpretation of what had occurred is given in the Biblical text in two poems; the Song of Miriam (Exodus 15 : 21) and the Song of Moses (15 : 1–18). These poems, both dating from a time before the reign of David, emphasize three things: The victory at the Sea was the Lord's, and the glory of it belongs to Him alone; the motive for His action was His "steadfast love" for His people; the strength and salvation of the people was to be found in their allegiance to Him.

The Covenant at Sinai

The formation of the nation took place at Mt. Sinai by the establishment of the covenant between the Lord and Israel (*Reference* Exodus 19 : 1–24 : 18).

The word "covenant" is fundamental to Biblical thought. It appears on the title page of every Bible, somewhat disguised in the translation "Testament". The two divisions of the Bible, then, are two "covenants", the old and the new. Basically the word simply means a legally binding agreement entered into by two contracting parties.

Such contracts can be of two main types. Sometimes the parties to the agreement stand on approximately equal footing and, therefore, each of them makes an agreement to do something of benefit to the other. Contracts of this kind may be called "parity covenants". A parity covenant between God and man is by definition an impossibility, since the two contracting parties can never face each other in terms of equality. The Sinai experience of Israel is, therefore, given in terms of the second type of contract, "the royal covenant". Here the two parties are unequal in status; one is master and lord; the other, subject and servant. The subject pledges himself to loyalty and obedience, and his duties and obligations are spelled out in detail. The royal party to the agreement pledges himself to nothing except that he will be king. He retains his freedom of action and is bound by no specific laws or rules. Into a covenant of this kind God invited the Israelites to enter at Mt. Sinai.

As much as this could be derived from the Old Testament itself, but immense help in understanding the nature of the Sinai covenant has been made available by the discovery of the Hittite royal treaties. These documents give the form of the agreement entered into between the Hittite kings and their vassal states, and this form was quite evidently adopted by the Israelites as an appropriate one in which to express the relationship between their nation and God.

From about 1500 to 1200 B.C. the Hittites were a major power. Their capital city in the mountains of Asia Minor was the centre of a large empire formed by conquest and alliance. The influence of the Hittites was felt far south of their geographical centre, and people of this nationality were an important component element in the mixed population of pre-Israelite Palestine.

The treaties by which the Hittite kings attempted to ensure the allegiance of their allies had a well-defined literary form. The first element in the treaty was an historical summary of the dealing of the king with the vassal, told in such a way as to emphasize the goodness of the king and his many acts of benevolence towards the weaker state. Then followed the stipulation of the duties of the vassal. The covenant law was thus set in the context of the kindness of the king, and the vassal was asked to accept it in grateful recognition of what the king had done for him. The legal sections of the covenant led to certain provisions for the safekeeping of the treaty, usually by placing it in a sacred place. The witnesses to the covenant were then listed, and the document ended with curses on those who break the covenant and blessings for those who maintain it.

The Divine King's Treaty

We are now able to see in a new light what has been happening in the exodus narrative. The account of the deliverance from Egypt is in effect an expanded historical summary of the divine king's dealing with Israel, told in such a way as to show the graciousness, kindness, and might of the Lord. It is the same type of preparation for the giving of the law as that found in the Hittite treaties, and its aim is to ensure that when Israel accepts the covenant she will do so in grateful recognition of the goodness of the Lord which made the covenant possible.

It is often said that the Old Testament is a religion of Law, while the New is the religion of Grace. Or, to put the same thing in another way, that the God of the Old Testament is a stern judge, while that of the New is a loving Father. The covenant form of the revelation at Sinai forces us to recognize that the Law is not the first element in Old Testament religion. The basic fact is God's deliverance of the people from slavery, and the law is represented as a gift given to Israel because of the kindly regard of God for her.

The Jewish custom of reading "I am the Lord, your God, who brought you out of the land of Egypt, out of the house of bondage", as the first commandment is more in keeping with the spirit of the Old Testament than is the Christian custom of omitting this sentence. The commandments are to be obeyed not for their own sake, but in gratitude to the God who found the people helpless in slavery, and brought them out of the house of bondage.

The later elements of the Hittite treaty form are also present and important in the exodus narrative. The tablets of the law were kept in the sacred ark. The covenant was renewed in an annual ceremony. The nation and the Lord were solemnly invoked as witnesses to it. And the blessing and curses consequent on obedience or disobedience were clearly expressed. In spirit, too, the Sinai covenant reflects the treaty form. There is the same exclusive claim of the divine king on the obedience of his subjects ("You shall have no other gods before me"), the same demand for voluntary obedience ("Choose you this day whom you will serve"), and the same sense that the destiny of the nation was determined by the choice.

The Nation at Sinai

The complicated literary structure of the Sinai story shows the importance which later generations attached to what happened there. When the nation was formed at the sacred mountain all its basic institutions were given to it by revelation from God. Everything that could be traced back to Sinai had a unique divine sanction and was an indispensable part of Israel. However, history does not stand still, and new occasions not only teach new duties, but also create new situations. Were the new ways of doing things less sacred or less vitally Israelite than the old? Israel answered this question by reading its more recent traditions back into the revelation at Sinai and by representing them, too, as given under divine authority when the nation was born.

This is not deliberate falsification of historical facts. Something like it happens with every society or club. The original "Constitution and By-laws" become antiquated as the association grows in numbers and assumes new responsibilities, but the

45

amendments become part of the original charter and have the same status as if they had existed from the beginning.

It will not be necessary to analyse the stories into their early and later strands, but the reader of the book of Exodus should be alert to their presence and should know why the complications exist. He should note especially the extensive priestly tradition which has been grafted into the Mosaic revelation (for example, Exodus 25: 1–31: 18).

Mount Sinai, modern Jebel Musa near the southern tip of the Arabian Peninsula, is a spectacular location for the great events associated with it. Towering above the rugged landscape of one of the most inhospitable deserts on earth, it gives the impression of loneliness, grandeur, and austere beauty. The Old Testament writers have heightened the effect of the natural splendour by picturing the mountain covered with dense cloud, echoing with thunder and bright with flashes of lightning, and with the sound of the trumpet echoing from its summit over the desert. Its sacred slopes were marked off so that neither animals nor men could wander into the presence of God.

As in the case of the march through the wilderness, these accompaniments may be explained as "natural". Perhaps the mountain was volcanic, and the overstimulated imagination of a primitive people created the idea of a god dwelling in the cloud and smoke. To read the story in this way is to miss its essential meaning. Each of the symbols is deliberately and carefully chosen to inform the reader that the nation has come into the authentic presence of God. Concealed from them, and maintaining the freedom of His own action, He was there in full authority and power, calling the people to a great assembly in which He would reveal His will and purpose to them and make them a nation dedicated to obedience and service to His law.

Moses, the mediator between God and Israel, ascended the mountain to receive the terms of the covenant from God.

The question of what law was given to Moses on the mountain is almost impossible to answer because so much later legislation has been brought into the Sinai context. However, the opinions of many scholars and the Biblical traditions themselves agree that the original form of the famous Ten Commandments is derived from Moses.

The Ten Laws

This brief legal code (Exodus 20: 1–17) is without parallel in the literature of the world. In the space of ten short sentences it provides the basis of Israel's religious and social life and deals with the inner attitude of the individual Israelite on which obedience to the law depends. In a religion which passed from tribal league to monarchy and eventually to world religion, the original law inevitably needed a great deal of expansion and interpretation. Nevertheless, every later stage of Israelite law is consciously dependent for its inspiration upon the Ten Commandments.

The first three laws regulate the *practice of religion*. They do not deny the existence of other gods, but they insist that within Israel the Lord, and He only, is to be worshipped. In this worship there is to be no attempt to represent Him in any visible form, or to identify Him with the forces of nature or with anything in the natural world. His name, by which the Hebrew language means the power of His nature, is not to be used in connection with any worthless, empty, or vain circumstance. This latter commandment is not fundamentally a prohibition against profanity. It is rather a condemnation of any attempt to debase religion to serve one's own ends. It applies far more to the man who goes to church in order to make good business contacts than to the man who says, "O Lord!" when he hits his finger with the hammer.

The three commandments regulating religion have two elements in common.

First, they emphasize the separateness and "otherness" of the God of Israel from any other being in the universe. He cannot be understood or described in terms of anything else, for there is nothing else like Him. We are often asked to "define God". In the light of the exodus tradition this is an impossibility. The

47

first problem of definition is to state to what class the object to be defined belongs. God belongs to no class. He stands in majestic isolation, a unique being. Hence the Old Testament tells us nothing about what God is like in Himself. To do this would be to penetrate a privacy and a mystery essentially impenetrable. What the Old Testament will do, and does with a richness that captures the imagination of its readers, is to describe how God, out of the mystery which belongs to Himself alone, acts towards men and on the scene of human history.

Secondly, the religious commandments reinforce the exclusive nature of the Lord's demands on His people. His will was the absolute authority to which they were bound, and the nation was thus constituted as a theocracy, a community ruled by the deity. All human leaders, whether kings, nobles, or priests, held their offices from Him and were subject to obedience to His law.

Worship of the Nation

The religious ordinances are followed by a single law regulating *formal worship*. The Sabbath, accordingly, appears as the basic religious institution of Israel, and the principle of the sacred seventh unit of time was extended in later legislation to years and weeks of years. The seventh day, the seventh year (the sabbatical year), and the fiftieth year (the Year of Jubilee) were sacred times; that is, they were "separate" from all secular time, their separateness being marked by the exclusion from them of any of the normal occupations and business concerns that fill the ordinary working day. The Sabbath is often, and rightly, justified on humanitarian grounds. The human being is not capable of uninterrupted labour unless time is provided for the rest of the body and the refreshment of the mind. But the Sabbath also expressed in a highly effective symbol the lordship of God over time. The use of the day as a time for commemoration of the exodus (Deuteronomy 5: 15) ensured that Israel would always be kept mindful of her slave origin and of the fact that she owed her existence to the liberating power of her God.

The other reason given for the observation of the Sabbath is that to refrain from work on the seventh day is to imitate the action of God, who rested on that day after the labour of creation. The Sabbath rest is only the special instance of a most important Biblical principle. The duty of the worshipper is to reflect in his conduct the activity which he ascribes to God. The prophetic demands for justice, righteousness, and love between Israelite and Israelite were based not on a theory of society, but on the conviction that because God acted in this way towards Israel, the people should express the same qualities in their dealings with one another.

The Nation's Social Institutions

The fifth to the ninth commandments preserve the integrity of the *social institutions* of Israel. They reflect the Hebrew conviction that the health of society depends on the family, and they safeguard the family by the demand for honour to parents and the prohibition against adultery. The sanctity of human life and inviolability of private property are also regarded as corner stones of society, and murder and theft are outlawed. No society can endure if it permits corruption in its legal system. Since Hebrew law permitted conviction on the testimony of two witnesses it was vital that the witnesses, in whose hands such power rested, should be scrupulously honest.

Murders, thefts, fornication, and corruption in the courts are the symptoms of a disease in society, but are not the disease itself. To find the infection one has to go beyond criminal acts to the *criminal mentality* from which the acts arise. This the tenth commandment attempts to do. Coveteousness, that attitude of self-centredness which ruthlessly seeks to get what it wants regardless of the rights or needs of others, is the direct opposite of the true spirit of Israel in which service and obedience to God should supersede self-gratification. In prohibiting covetousness the Ten Commandments put forth a law which no policeman can enforce. Strictly speaking it is not law at all but a statement of the psychological condition which produces lawlessness. It is, however, essential in the stipulations of the Israelite covenant. The nation is conceived as a legal unit, responsible not to the authority of the people through the machinery of the democratic vote, but responsible to a God who can see and weigh, not only the action, but the motive as well.

Expansion of the Laws

The Ten Commandments probably existed first in the form of ten very brief prohibitions. These were soon expanded by the addition of explanatory sentences, and two slightly different versions were eventually produced (Exodus 20: 1–17, Deuteronomy 5: 6–21). During the period of the Judges a much longer legal code was developed, still in the spirit of the Ten Commandments but drawing on the common law of the ancient Near East for many of its specific rules. This was called "The Book of the Covenant" and is inserted in *Exodus* as part of the revelation given to Moses on Mt. Sinai (chapter 20: 21–23: 33). This is a simple code for an agricultural people, with no mention of a king and little recognition of a merchant class. It begins with a statement of the nature of God and a description of the altar to be used in His worship (20: 21–26). It then elaborates the Ten Commandments by spelling out the punishment in specially selected criminal cases and prescribing the penalty. It regulates slavery (21: 2–11), legislates for the observance of the Sabbaths and the festivals (23: 10–19), and emphasizes the spirit of justice and humane conduct that ought to prevail in Israel (22: 21–23: 9).

A further expansion of the covenant law, drawn up this time in the interests of the priests and the formal religion which they administered, concludes the book of Exodus (25: 1–31: 18; 35: 1–40: 38). The main themes of this priestly legislation, the ark, the tabernacle, and the priesthood, will be dealt with in the next chapter.

Hebrew law, and especially the Ten Commandments, is often

criticized on the grounds that it is negative, and the "thou shalt not's" of the Old Testament are compared unfavourably with the "law of love" in the New Testament. The negative quality of law is, however, essential in the preservation of liberty. The law sets the limits beyond which one cannot go, and within the boundaries thus drawn the individual is free to regulate his own conduct. To set down a positive law is at once to cut off all lines of action but one. The achievement of the Ten Commandments in setting the essential limits of conduct in so brief a compass is a marvel of economy and precision.

A second censure sometimes directed at Old Testament law is that it is not original but borrows from other ancient codes. There was, indeed, much legal activity in the ancient Near East, and we possess codes of law from Sumer dating as early as 2150 B.C. as well as the famous code of Hammurabi (about 1700 B.C.). Striking parallels can be drawn between these codes and Old Testament law. The parallels fall mostly in regulations known as case law. This type of legislation has the form "If (followed by the details of a particular legal situation), then (followed by the proper settlement of the case)". Such laws are the accumulated experience of many generations of legal practice, and the Hebrews often adopted them from the legal tradition shared by many Semitic peoples.

Another type of law is more blunt and direct, having the form of a direct word of God, "Thou shalt . . .", or "Thou shalt not . . ." These "apodictic" laws are the heart of the terms of the covenant. In them the reader can recognize what is most distinctively Israelite, and, by giving special attention to them, see what are the most critical demands of the covenant into which Israel entered.

The covenant presented by Moses was accepted by the free choice of the people, and their acceptance was sealed by the sprinkling of the blood of a sacrificial animal on the people and by a common meal (Exodus 24: 1–11). In this act of ratification the relationship between God and Israel was permanently established, and the nation in all its essentials was formed.

51

Israel had been brought face to face with an austere and mighty God whose inner nature was concealed from their knowledge, but who, moved by the suffering of an enslaved people, entered into the stream of historical events to deliver them from bondage and to make them His own people by offering them His covenant. They now formally recognized their complete dependence on this God of deliverance, and bound themselves to live in exclusive obedience to His law. "All that the Lord has spoken we will do, and we will be obedient" (Exodus 24: 7). This sentence, seen against the background of the exodus from Egypt and the nature of a covenant relationship, is the constitution of Israel, the secret of its individuality as a nation, and the well-spring of its continuing influence in human history.

5

DISCIPLINE OF THE DESERT

Reference Numbers 10: 1—21: 25

AFTER THE formation of the nation by the Sinai covenant the intention was to march directly to Canaan and, under the protection and guidance of the Lord, to conquer and occupy the land. To this end Israel moved from Sinai in a north-easterly direction to the northern tip of the Gulf of Aqabah, and thence north-west to Kadesh-Barnea, directly south of the west Jordan region of Palestine, in position to strike directly into the heart of the promised land, the region which later became the Kingdom of Judah. Details of this and the later itinerary of Israel are provided mainly by the P source. (Numbers 10: 1–24: 25).

At the command of the Lord, who through Moses had directed the entire operation, twelve spies were sent out to reconnoitre the invasion route. Their report was a mixture of hopefulness and pessimism. The land was a fine prize of war, fertile and full of prosperous cities, but it was defended by massive fortifications manned by skilled warriors. Caleb and Joshua advised immediate attack. Since the victory would be won by the Lord the formidable strength of the enemy and the relative weakness of Israel were of no significance. This view was not shared by the majority of the people, who "murmured" against Moses and Aaron, and preferred to return to slavery than to begin an unequal battle for possession of the land.

The contrasting attitudes of Caleb and Joshua on the one hand and the people on the other are instances of two points of view which appear repeatedly in the exodus narrative. The advice of the two spies to attack, ignoring the odds, belongs to the ideology of the Holy War. The reluctance of the people to trust the Lord for victory is a striking example of the "murmuring tradition". By considering these in detail here we will be setting up the background for understanding and interpreting many other parts of the exodus story which are dominated by the same ideas.

The "Holy War" Tradition

The Holy War is an ancient tradition if Israel. It depends on the theological premise that "the Lord is a man of war" (Exodus 15: 3). In carrying out His purpose in history the God of Israel may decree a war, and, when He does so, it is the *religious* duty of His people to make ready their armies for battle. The troops are assembled at the command of God, given through His prophets or chosen representatives. In all its details the strategy of the war is determined by the Lord, and, when the battle is joined, the terror of God falls on the enemy and leaves him powerless to offer effective resistance. This is what Caleb and Joshua say of the Canaanites, "Their protection is removed from them, and the Lord is with us" (Numbers 14: 9), and this is why, when the Israelites later attack without the command of God, they are disastrously defeated by the Amalekites and Canaanites (14: 45).

Since victory in the Holy War is not won by the swords or bows of the Israelites, but by the power of God, complete faith in the ability of God to win the victory is more important than military training, numbers, or equipment. The famous incident of the reduction of Gideon's army from thirty-two thousand to three hundred by the elimination of the fearful and the careless is a case in point (Judges 7: 1–18). In fact the Lord prefers the smaller force in order that there may be no possibility of attributing the victory to human prowess.

Since God wins the victory, the spoils of war belong to Him. Human beings, animals, buildings, and equipment were totally destroyed as a sacrifice to the Victor-God. The completeness of the destruction required by the Holy War may be seen in the barbarity with which the Midianites were treated after their defeat at the hands of the Israelites (Numbers 31). Stories of this kind are among the most disturbing passages in the Old Testament. It is impossible to condone the savagery of these actions, but the ideology of the Holy War enables us to understand why brutality of this type was regarded as a religious duty in ancient Israel.

At risk of disrupting the chronological order of our presentation, it may be well to bring in at this point some of the more prominent cases of the Holy War from both before and after the incident of the spies.

The first occurrence of Holy War ideology is in the battle of Israel against the Amalekites shortly after the people had left Egypt. The determining factor in the struggle was the power of the Lord, mediated through the outstretched hands of Moses. Aaron and Hur had to hold up Moses' hands or Israel, despite her best efforts, would have been defeated (Exodus 17: 8–13).

The battles fought along the east bank of the Dead Sea against the Midianites and related people are full of Holy War ideas (Numbers 20: 1–22: 1; 31: 1–54). The quaint story of Balaam and his talking ass belongs in this category (Numbers 22: 2–24: 25). The secret weapon of ancient armies was not the rocket or the H-bomb, but the professional curser. Some men were unusually close to the deity, and possessed an extraordinary measure of divine power. This they could gather up and fling at an enemy in the form of a curse. Accordingly, before two armies clashed the cursers on each side would shout their anathemas against the enemy, and the side with the strongest curser might win the battle before a sword was drawn.

Balaam, a redoubtable curser, was hired by Balak, the king of Moab, to oppose the Israelites. The Biblical account leaves no doubt of Balaam's capacity. "He whom you bless is blessed, and he whom you curse is cursed" (Numbers 22: 6). If Balaam came into action, Israel was doomed. But (and this is the main point of the story) the power of the Lord in the Holy War is so great that, when Balaam opens his mouth to curse Israel, he utters a blessing. The words of the blessings are ancient poems predicting the future greatness of Israel (Numbers 23: 7–10, 18–24; 24: 3–9, 15–24).

The struggles of the Judges to maintain control of the land against the pressure of successive invasions move in the atmosphere of Holy War, and the best sustained illustration of its operation is the call of Gideon, and the campaigns conducted under his leadership (Judges 6–8).

Early Israel had no spirit of pacifism or brotherly love towards its enemies. The people served a warrior God and at His command they conducted ruthless total war against the enemy. The Christian will rightly insist that the Holy War is based on a false conception of the nature of God and a misunderstanding of His revelation. Nevertheless, the complete trust in the sufficiency of God, and the selfless devotion to His purposes required by the Holy War, when stripped of their warlike and brutal qualities, became a permanent part of the Judeo-Christian tradition.

Caleb and Joshua stood firmly in the tradition of the Holy War. The people to whom they presented their report rejected the idea of the Holy War at precisely its crucial point. They refused to trust God for victory in the face of the odds against success, and they "murmured" against their own leaders and against God.

The "Murmuring" Tradition

The complaint of the people began early in the period of the wilderness wanderings. The murmuring at the Red Sea was only quelled by Moses' vigorous speech, "The Lord will fight for you" (Exodus 14: 10–18). Once in the wilderness and short of food and water, the people denounced Moses as a false leader, "Would that we had died by the hand of the Lord in the land of Egypt, when we sat by the fleshpots and ate bread to the full; for you have brought us out into this wilderness to kill this whole assembly with hunger" (Exodus 16: 3). Moses' response sharply states the vital issue at stake. "Your murmurings are not against us but against the Lord" (16: 8). On this occasion the

Lord responded by satisfying the demand of the people with manna and quails.

Somewhat later, and in the very centre of the Sinai revelation, the murmuring reappeared in a more serious form. While Moses was in conversation with God upon the mountain, the people, impatient at the long delay and fearing that Moses was dead, insisted that Aaron make them other gods. The golden calf was the result, and the consequence of this apostasy was a destructive plague (Exodus 32).

In the case of Israel's refusal to attack Canaan in response to the report of the spies the penalty was even more drastic. So that none of the murmurers would see the promised land, the nation was condemned to remain in the wilderness until the whole of the apostate generation, except the two faithful spies, had died.

Still later Korah, abetted by certain others, protested against the autocratic rule of Moses and Aaron. Their reasons appear quite sound to a democratically-minded reader. The rebels argued that the whole nation was holy to the Lord, and that, therefore, its members stood on terms of equality, and it was against the covenant that two men should have such absolute power. The democratic principle is not, however, the foundation of Israel's covenant constitution. The protest of Korah is a protest against the right of the Lord to rule Israel as He sees fit. The rebellion is punished by the destruction of its leaders, and by the death of many Israelites in a plague.

The most conspicuous feature of the people's attitude, as reflected in their murmuring, is a desire to be permanently successful without personal discomfort or pain. As soon as difficulties arise the murmuring begins. The nation is quite evidently religious for what it can "get out" of its religion. Its own welfare is its chief concern, and whenever that welfare is threatened it casts about for someone on whom to put the blame. This is the opposite of the spirit of the covenant. In effect, it makes God the servant of Israel, rather than Israel the servant of God. Only on this premise could the nation feel that, when its affairs began to go badly, its God had failed, and it was free to choose other gods and other leaders, who might be more successful in looking after its well-being.

Compounding the self-centredness out of which the murmurings came was a lack of confidence in the power of the Lord. Even after the deliverance from Egypt the people were never really sure that their God was competent to overcome the immense difficulties that confronted them in the bleak wilderness and against the powerful armies of Canaan. The mind of the nation was given to calculating the odds on the basis of hard facts which they could see and weigh. The imponderable in the situation, the sovereignty of their God over the historical process, impressed them less than the size and strength of the opposition, or hunger pains in their stomachs.

The reason for dwelling so long on the murmuring tradition is twofold. First, it is a recurrent theme of the stories themselves, and, second, it has far-reaching implications for the later development of Old Testament faith. The prophetic movement, to take only one example, is motivated by the conviction that the state of mind of the murmurers meant national destruction, and its opposite, as represented by Caleb and Joshua, contained the only hope for the survival of Israel. Hence, the great operative word of prophetic theology is trust, for on it depended the life or death of the covenant community.

The murmuring tradition also brings into clear focus the Old Testament philosophy of history. In the Old Testament human events are taken seriously for the first time as the arena in which God acts and in which He reveals His purpose and brings it to reality. Therefore, the will of God is the formative element in the affairs of men, and in the end the record of history will show the triumph of the divine purpose. If God wills that Israel shall inhabit Canaan, to that land she will eventually come. But the will of God is not the only will operative in history. Human purposes have their place and power. When the human will is bent to the service of the purpose of God, events move constructively and progressively forward. When, however, the human will is set to serve its own ends, and when the well-being of the human community is set above faithfulness to the divine purpose, confusion and disaster result. The succession of plagues by which the murmurers were devastated, and the prohibition of the rebels from entering Canaan, are graphic symbols of this view of history. The changes and disasters to which man is subject are, in the Biblical view, the evidence of his failure to recognize that his destiny depends on his willingness to bring his own will into conformity with the will of God in the attitude of trust.

The Priests and their Duties

The accounts of the wilderness wanderings in Exodus and Numbers contain a great deal of material dealing with the priesthood. This is of three kinds—stories about priests, such as the bloodthirsty account of the zeal of Phinehas (Numbers 25), laws governing the priestly office, such as the laws of sacrifice (Numbers 28: 1–29: 40), and descriptions of priestly institutions, such as the ark and the tabernacle (Exodus 25: 10–22; 26: 1–37). Many modern readers are impatient with the masses of detail about customs and practices altogether foreign to their experience, and they are inclined to skip all these sections as unimportant or unintelligible. But the priesthood and its duties was an integral part of Israel from earliest times to the destruction of the city of Jerusalem by the Romans in A.D. 70, and an institution of such centrality and long duration deserves some attempt to understand its aims and reason for existence.

The charter of the priesthood is the holiness of God, and the corresponding necessity that the nation bound to Him in covenant should also be holy. The priests, therefore, had two main functions. The first was *to preserve and to teach the law*. It was only by knowledge of the will of God that the nation could serve and obey Him. The priests operated the "system" of public education in ancient Israel. They interpreted and explained the terms of the covenant to the people, and exhorted them to obedience. When an individual had a problem of morals or conduct he came to the priests for an answer, and received a "direction". The Hebrew word for "direction" (*torah*) eventually became the descriptive word for Law, and when the Torah is read on the Sabbath in the synagogue worship the combined efforts of generations of priests in the preservation and interpretation of the Law is being tacitly acknowledged fifty generations after the priesthood had ceased to function.

The second, and more characteristic, task of the priest was, in the Biblical language, "*to make a distinction between the clean and the unclean.*" No form of uncleanness could be allowed to exist in the presence of the Holy God. If the nation became contaminated with impurity its holiness was in peril, and its qualification to belong to the God of holiness was destroyed. Uncleanness might be of a ritual kind, such as impurity from touching a dead body, or from contact with blood. It might also be moral, arising from rebellion against the God of the covenant. The distinction between these two forms of uncleanness was not sharply drawn. Both rendered the nation impure and incapable of serving the God of holiness.

The priests claimed no power to remove the ultimate source of uncleanness. They could not cure leprosy or forgive sin. What they could do was to remove the stain of impurity left after the source of uncleanness had been removed. They could, through the sacrificial system, take away the guilt of sin repented and forgiven, or remove from a leper the impurity remaining when his disease had been cured.

The purification ritual consisted of three elements: a waiting period of a day, a week, or several weeks after the source of contamination had been removed, treatment with a purifying agent such as water, blood, or a liquid compounded of several cleansing materials, and a sacrifice of the nature of a sin offering.

With this background the two main blocks of purity laws in the book of Numbers may be better understood (*References*: Numbers 5: 1–6: 27; 19: 1–22). One odd aspect of the priestly office which shows up in these laws is the detective responsibilities of the priests. By a complex and terrifying ritual they acted in cases of suspected adultery (Numbers 5: 11–31), and of murder committed in the absence of witnesses (Deuteronomy 21).

The priests, thus, combined the offices of educator, physician, lawyer, judge, and police officer. In some of these functions the secular judges and elders shared, but at any point where the holiness of Israel was threatened by ignorance, impurity, or sin, the priest was called into action. Everything he did expressed the two-sided nature of his task. Through his instruction and preaching of the law he brought the will of God before the people. When he presided at the altar, presenting the offerings of the worshippers, he conducted the people into the presence of God, where they might remember their origin in slavery, and renew their allegiance to the covenant on which the nation was founded.

The prophet was more spectacular, more incisive, more compelling than the priest, but who is to say whether in the work-a-day job of instruction and worship the priests did not do as much as the prophets to hold the nation together and to maintain its witness to the authentic nature of its faith?

Origin of the Priesthood

On the question of the origin of the priesthood Israelite tradition is not firm. Moses' father-in-law, Jethro, offered sacrifices to the Lord (Exodus 18) while Moses stood by. Aaron was with Moses from the beginning and the priestly functions were clearly concentrated in his hands, but in addition the entire tribe of Levi was ordained to the priesthood and had priestly offices. Notably the Levites were accepted by the Lord instead of the sacrifice of the first-born children from all tribes, and were given a status of special holiness because of this fact (Numbers 3: 1–13). The complexity of the problem is undoubtedly caused by the telescoping of the long history of the priesthood into the Mosaic period, and representing successive stages of the development as if they had been in existence from the beginning. The course of events may be reconstructed with a fair degree of probability. In the Mosaic period the office of the priest was most likely not confined to any special class. Moses, Jethro, or Aaron could offer sacrifices on behalf of the nation, and in the smaller circle of the family the father acted as priest. After the settlement in Canaan the powers of the priesthood were concentrated in the hands of the Levites, but as time went on this group became too large, and the effective priesthood was confined to the descendants of Aaron, with the Levites retaining only the minor functions of Temple servants and singers.

Although the history may be unclear, the basic ideas of the priesthood are given with uncomfortable bluntness in the story of Phinehas (*Reference*: Numbers 25). An Israelite was seen going into his tent with a foreign woman. Phinehas rose from worship in front of the Tabernacle and, rushing into the tent, drove his spear through the belly of both offenders. For this "zealous" action he was awarded a covenant of perpetual priesthood for himself and his family.

Phinehas' action was motivated by an intense desire to keep Israel pure from any contaminating influence, and he went to the extreme in carrying out this purpose. Phinehas is a portrait of zeal for the purity of Israel drawn larger than life. He, therefore, is properly the prototype and founding father of the priesthood.

Phinehas is said to have shown a zeal like the zeal of the Lord. The Hebrew word rendered "zeal" is often translated "jealousy", and appears in the well-known description of God, "I the Lord your God am a jealous God" (Exodus 20: 5). The basic meaning of the word is "to become red" (from intensity of passion). Used of God, it means that He is never casual or indifferent to the actions of His people, but responds with vigour to their disobedience by "visiting the iniquities of the fathers upon the children," and with equal intensity to their faithfulness by "showing steadfast love to thousands." The same kind of seriousness and complete abandon in action, appearing in Phinehas, qualified him to receive the covenant of perpetual priesthood.

The priesthood, like the nation, was formed by a covenant.

A binding agreement was established between God and the family of Phinehas which was to last forever. In this respect the priestly covenant differs from the national. At Sinai the nation had an either/or written across its contract. Obedience brought the blessings of the covenant, but disobedience meant disaster and destruction. No such a condition appeared in the covenant with Phinehas. It belonged to him and his children, whether they were faithful or untrue, in perpetuity. The covenant with the nation, therefore, remained the fundamental agreement. Within the structure of the covenant people, permanent institutions such as that of the priesthood (and later, on much the same terms, the monarchy) could be set up. But they stood or fell with the survival of the nation, and that, in its turn, depended unequivocally on obedience.

Covenant law prevented the Israelite priesthood from representing the Lord by any image or idol. The tradition, however, retained the memory of two important religious symbols which had existed in the desert period: the *Tent of Meeting* or *Tabernacle,* and the *Ark of the Covenant.* The Biblical description of both these sacred objects comes from late priestly sources and has been influenced by ideas that arose much later than the desert period.

The Tent of Meeting

The Tent of Meeting was probably an ordinary goat's hair tent, a little richer than the usual dwelling, but of the same style and construction. It stood outside the camp, where the holiness associated with it would not endanger the people. The Lord was present in this tent, and, when the nation wished to consult Him on any matter, it gathered in the open space in front of the structure to hear the word of the Lord mediated through Moses.

The priestly tradition elaborated this simple dwelling tent into a portable replica in acacia wood and leather of the later Temple of Jerusalem, and provided it with all the equipment of a large and permanent shrine; an offering table, a lamp stand, two altars, and a brass wash-basin. The priestly writers also made a significant change in its location. Whereas the primitive tradition placed it outside the camp, the priestly documents located it in the centre. The Levites pitched their tents around it to serve it and to keep the profane tribes at a distance, and each of the other tribes had its assigned position surrounding the Tabernacle. In this way the priests expressed a conviction, present in all their literature, that the whole life of the nation ought to be organized and ordered around the place of worship.

The Ark of the Covenant

The ark was an oblong wooden box about three by two feet fitted with two handles so that it could be carried somewhat like a sedan chair, and covered with gold inside and out. It had a golden lid, called the "mercy seat", and two golden cherubs (creatures with an animal body and a human face) seated on either side with their wings outspread over the ark. Inside were placed a collection of sacred objects, among them the tablets of the Law. This portable shrine was in reality an empty throne, the seat formed by the wings of the cherubs and the footstool by the "mercy seat". In camp the ark rested in the Tent; on the march it was carried by the Levites in the forefront of the column.

The ark was a fitting symbol of the God of the covenant. From His throne on the wings of the cherubs above the mercy seat the divine king communed with His people. At his feet lay the Law, a continual challenge to the nation to remember the covenant. It was most appropriate, however, to a wandering people—the portable symbol of a travelling god—and when the Israelites settled in Canaan its influence gradually declined.

It was given a permanent home in the shrine at Shiloh, and, when the Philistines demolished that sacred place, it remained in a private home until David brought it up to Jerusalem. Under the monarchy the Temple and its altars replaced the ark as Israel's chief religious symbol, and it is rarely mentioned after the time of Solomon. Presumably it perished in the destruction of the Temple by the Babylonians in 586 B.C.

The Nation Hardened and Unified

After the cowardly reception of the spies' report, the nation, condemned to forty years in the wilderness, wandered in the mountainous and barren territory south of the Dead Sea. When the time of their waiting was over and a new generation, hardened and unified by desert life, was ready to move against Canaan, the tribes abandoned the old plan of striking due north into Palestine, and marched around the east side of the Dead Sea. The way was blocked by the kingdoms of Edom and Moab, which had come into existence only about 1300 B.C. Being refused passage through these kingdoms, they circled out into the desert and by-passed the hostile territory.

When, however, they came north of the River Arnon they were within the bounds of the land promised to them, and, under the generalship of Moses, they subdued the Amorite king, Sihon, and his northern neighbour Og, King of Bashan, a gigantic man who left as his memorial only a huge iron bed (Numbers 21: 21–35). Israel, thus, came into the possession of a considerable tract of land east of the Jordan, which was assigned to the tribes of Reuben, Gad, and half Manasseh.

The first acts of the drama of Israel's history have now been unfolded. God has revealed Himself to the people, broken the Egyptian hold upon them, led them into the wilderness, offered them His covenant, and disciplined them by hard years of desert life. It remains only for Israel to cross the river Jordan and enter into her heritage.

6

INTO THE PROMISED LAND

Reference Joshua 1: 1—12: 24; Judges 1: 1—2: 5

It is often pointed out that there are two accounts of the conquest of Canaan in the Old Testament. The first, which may be called the "triumphal procession theory", is found in Joshua 1: 1–12: 24. It pictures the Israelites under the command of Joshua marching through the land in uninterrupted conquest. The enemies are easily defeated, the cities taken, and the land annexed to the possessions of Israel. When the whole of Canaan has been conquered, the land is divided among the tribes, the tribal boundaries are fixed, and the Levites, who get no land, are provided for from the revenues of certain cities (Joshua 13: 1–24: 33). At one stroke Canaan passes into Israelite hands, and the covenant people receive the promised land as a gift from their God, for His might, not their own strength, accomplished the conquest.

Historically, this account does not ring true. It appears to have been written long after the events, in terms of the strict theory of the Holy War. There are some early elements in it, but the main outline of the story is the work of priestly theoreticians.

The much briefer account in Judges 1: 1–2: 5, happily called "the piecemeal account", has a greater ring of factuality. It shows the Israelites fighting their way into the land as separate tribal groups. They meet with varied success. Some are able to occupy the land into which they come, and even have considerable success against the fortified cities. Other tribes are able only to infiltrate the hill country, and can do nothing against the towns in the valleys. They are forced to settle down side by side with the native Canaanite population. Still others can make no headway at all, and must select another point of attack against less well defended, but less valuable, territory. According to this account, the conquest was a protracted affair, extending over a considerable period of time, and the native population was only slowly brought under Israelite control.

Conquest and Coalition

Archaeological discoveries of the last half century have made it impossible any longer to see the piecemeal and triumphal views of the conquest in sharp contrast. A series of cities in the southern hill country, and the great city of Hazor in Galilee, were all destroyed about the same time in the thirteenth century B.C. The location of these cities fits well with the description of Joshua's campaigns in the region. The major puzzle was Jericho, where early evidence indicated a destruction during the fifteenth century. More recent excavation has forced a revision of this view, since almost no trace of the Canaanite city remains on the site, and its destruction date cannot be established.

The evidence points to the conclusion that the battle-hardened invaders from the desert found in the hill country a native population related to them by blood and ready to form an alliance with them. The coalition thus formed made an immediate and successful attack on some of the cities in the region, and defeated an alliance of Canaanite cities under the ruler of Lachish. Against the wealthier and larger cities in the fertile valleys of the north they had, however, little or no success, and could only establish a foot-hold in the hills. Strong Canaanite influences thus survived in close proximity to the Israelite villages and towns.

The Tribal Structure

The tribes were organized as semi-independent units (Judges 5–11). They held to the common worship of the Lord, and venerated the ark and its shrine at Shiloh. Annually they renewed the covenant in a ceremony at Shechem, and they were pledged to join in united Holy War at the threat of attack against any member of the league. Generally, however, only the tribes nearest the danger turned out in strength.

The Song of Deborah (Judges 5), actually composed in the period, gives a fascinating glimpse of this loose tribal structure. The Canaanites threatened to reassert their control of the land under their king, Jabin, and his general, Sisera. The prophetess Deborah called for a Holy War, and the Lord Himself marched from His mountain home to join the combat. Ephraim, Benjamin, Machir, Zebulun, Naphtali, and Issachar answered the call to arms, but Reuben, Gilead, Dan, and Asher sent no troops. The rest of the tribes are not mentioned, probably because they were too far from the scene of hostilities to be expected to take part. In the battle the Lord used the forces of nature to defeat the Canaanites, and their leader met an ignominious death at the hands of a peasant woman as he fled from the battle.

The loose tribal organization of Israel was continuously under pressure from other peoples who, like Israel, were trying to push into the territory of the Canaanites. The Moabites attempted to invade the land by way of Jericho, and were prevented when Ehud murdered their king (Judges 3). Midianites from the desert terrorized the populace with their plundering raids until Gideon put a stop to their marauding (Judges 6–8). The Ammonites attacked the trans-Jordanian possessions, and were put to the sword by Jephthah, who reflects the savage spirit of the age by sacrificing his daughter in fulfilment of his vow (Judges 11–12).

The Philistines

Towards the end of the period of the Judges (1200–1050 B.C.) a more formidable enemy began to intrude into Israelite territory. A group of Sea Peoples, racially related to the Greeks, attacked all along the Mediterranean coast and even attempted to invade Egypt. They were able to settle along the south coast of Palestine and by 1050 B.C. had a powerful league of five strong cities, and were sending their armies up the valleys into the hill country of central Palestine. The Israelite bronze sword was no match for the new iron weapons of the Philistines, and the heroic nuisance tactics of Samson had no practical results. It was clear that only a centralized government, probably a monarchy, could save Israel from the Philistine menace. The first stage of Israel's life in the promised land thus came to an end. The old tribal league, based on the sovereignty of the Lord and loyalty to the covenant, was doomed, and the way was open for the rise of Saul and David and the founding of the monarchy.

Conflict with Paganism

The period of the Judges was marked by a struggle between the religion of the desert and the native religion of Canaan. The exclusive worship of the Lord, and the stringent moral demands of the covenant, came into conflict with a paganism of many gods and a lax sexual morality condoned by the sanctions of religion. The principal Canaanite deity was Baal, Lord of the Storm and controller of the fertility of the soil. The myth and ritual associated with his worship included sacred prostitution, both male and female, as a means of stimulating the growth of the crops. Images, strictly prohibited in the desert religion, were a common feature of Canaanite religion, and the host of male and female deities venerated by the Canaanites were an affront to the claim that the Lord alone should be worshipped.

It was not as clear to the Israelite as it is to us that his religion was higher and better than the Canaanite. The religion of the land was practiced by sophisticated city dwellers much more skilled in the arts of civilization than the desert people. It had the attraction of novelty and of culture. In addition, the Lord was a god of war and of the desert and mountain. He might not be able to administer the affairs of an agricultural people, a task in which Baal had been tested for centuries. The simple ritual of the wilderness period looked poor beside the gaudy festivals of Canaan, and the stern disciplines of desert life were hard to maintain in the more comfortable environment of an agricultural town.

A battle began in these early days between Yahweh and Baal which continued throughout the entire period of the monarchy. The main task of the prophets was to continue the struggle now begun, and to insist on the principles of "The Lord alone", and the preservation of the covenant. The greatest danger was not that the Lord would be forgotten or His worship abandoned. The real peril was that He would be confused with Baal, the attributes of Baal given to Him, and His character subtly transformed from that revealed to Moses to something indistinguishable from a run-of-the-mill fertility deity.

The struggle can be seen taking shape in the story of Gideon (Judges 6: 25–32). Gideon's own father had erected an altar to Baal, and a sacred wooden pole (Asherah) near it. The destruction of these objects almost caused a riot in the village. The account clearly indicates the perilous position of the worship of the Lord in these confused times.

The baalistic religion of Canaan was associated with a tradition of hereditary kingship. A group of letters found in Egypt in the royal archives of Amenophis III and Amenophis IV (the Amarna Letters) show that many of the cities of Palestine were ruled by petty kings who owed allegiance to the Pharaoh, but did not adhere to it if there was any chance of asserting their independence. These letters date from about 1400 B.C., and indicate a royal tradition at least two hundred years old, but probably much older.

The "Judges" as Military Leaders

Hereditary kingship was completely repugnant to the covenant tradition. The Lord alone was king of Israel and He appointed leaders of His own choosing as the need arose. They were selected by God to meet a specific emergency, drew their power from Him, and held office only while the emergency lasted. The Old Testament calls them "Judges", but the legal connotations of the word are misleading. They were military leaders, rather than officers of a law court, and their function was to deliver the people from a foreign attacker.

Gideon (Judges 6–8) is a typical Judge. He was an ordinary farmer from one of the less prominent families of the tribe of Manasseh, and he was as fearful as anyone else in Israel of the dreaded Midianite raiders. An angel of the Lord came to him while he was "threshing wheat in a wine press to hide it from the Midianites", and commissioned him as the deliverer of Israel. He proved his devotion and courage by the destruction of the baalistic images, and when a coalition of Midianites and Amalekites crossed the Jordan, he summoned the armies and marched to battle.

At this point in the story a most important sentence occurs. "The Spirit of the Lord took possession of Gideon." The Spirit is the invisible power of God. When it enters a person all his natural capacities are lifted to superhuman heights, and he is able to accomplish feats of wisdom and courage impossible to an ordinary man. The Spirit of the Lord gave the Judge the power he needed to command the people. As long as it was upon him he was the invincible instrument of the Lord. When it left him he was an ordinary citizen once more. The technical term for this type of leadership is "charismatic", from the Greek *charisma*, "a gift". In her early days Israel depended on the "gifted" leadership. It was more native to the covenant community than kingship, because it left no doubt of the sovereignty of God over the nation, and because it made clear that the Judge's authority and powers were not his own, but were bestowed on him in the interest of the nation.

Armed with the *charisma* Gideon led the troops into battle in a typical Holy War. The army was pitifully small, three hundred against a multitude, but the surprise attack on the Midianite camp succeeded when "the Lord set every man's sword against his fellow" and the ensuing victory was complete.

The conflict between the royal and the charismatic concept of leadership comes to open expression when the people try to make Gideon king. Gideon's reply is a perfect expression of the tribal covenant tradition, "I will not rule over you, and my son will not rule over you; the Lord will rule over you."

His son, Abimelech, was not, however, of the same opinion. He accepted the crown from the men of Shechem, a city with a history of kingship going back to 1750 B.C. In his new office Abimelech was balanced on a razor's edge. A revolt by the same men of Shechem who had recently made him king was ruthlessly suppressed with the total destruction of the city, but Abimelech did not live long to enjoy his victory. In the siege of the neighbouring city of Thebez he got too near the wall, and was killed by a millstone dropped on his head by a brawny female defender of the city.

The contrasting cases of Gideon and Abimelech show the tension between conflicting theories of government in early Israelite Palestine. The conflict was never completely resolved. A strong current of opposition always existed in Israel against the kingship. The king's powers were regulated by law, and the prophets did not hesitate to speak against apostate or unworthy kings. But the book of Judges itself testifies to the need for the monarchy. The unedifying stories with which the book closes reveal a condition of near anarchy and virtual savagery (Judges 19–21). The editor is accurate in his summation of the situation. "In those days there was no king in Israel; every man did what was right in his own eyes" (21 : 25).

Defenders of the Covenant

In these troubled times groups were formed which in later Israelite history were the stoutest defenders of the covenant. The first mention of prophets in action is in Judges 5 : 1 and 6 : 8. Deborah, the prophetess, stood beside the Judge, Barak, rallying the tribes to fight the Canaanites, and at the time of the Midianite crisis an unnamed prophet warned the people against the dangers of idolatry.

Prophecy was not an Israelite invention. Pagan deities had

their spokesmen who announced their word to the people, and an Egyptian document, the Story of Wen-Amon, shows that prophets existed among the Phoenicians, a people closely related to the Canaanites. It is one of the ironies of history that the institution most vigorous in its opposition to Baalism was probably borrowed from the Canaanites themselves.

A less famous group than the prophets, the Nazirites, probably originated in this period. The Nazirite vow is given in Numbers 6: 2–21, and includes abstinence from wine and from cutting the hair or beard. The Nazirites were not tee-totallers on moral grounds. Wine was a characteristic product of agricultural civilization, and the well-trimmed hair and beard a mark of the city dweller. The Nazirite movement was in reality a protest in the name of the old desert tradition against the new life, centred in the field and the town. The Nazirite was regarded as a holy man, and a true representative of the covenant religion of Israel not only because of his vow, but because of his refusal to compromise the tribal, nomadic life in which the covenant had been given.

Samson was committed to the life of a Nazirite from his birth (Judges 13: 1–6). He conscientiously broke all the vows, going so far as to marry a Philistine woman. This uncouth child of a rugged age was attracted to the luxury of the Philistine cities, addicted to visiting prostitutes, and possessed of an ungovernable temper. In his self-centredness he wasted his gift of mighty strength, and his sporadic acts against the Philistines were motivated by desire for revenge, rather than for the liberation of Israel. In the end, blinded and alone, he was dragged to the temple of Dagon for the amusement of the Philistines on one of their festival days. With the memory of the wasted years in his mind and his heart full of anger for the loss of his eyes, he became for a moment a true Nazirite, a zealot for the Lord. He prayed, "Only this once", and with a last exertion of his strength brought the temple crashing down on the worshippers and himself.

Obedience Leads to Prosperity

Reference Judges 3 : 7—31

We have so far been reconstructing the history of the conquest and settlement of Canaan in as nearly factual terms as possible, and have been examining the religious and political crises of the period. The basis of the study has been the primitive stories of the Judges, and we have as yet paid little attention to the later framework in which the stories are set.

Examination of Judges 3 : 7–31 reveals a literary pattern which is repeated at many other points in the book. The people of Israel do evil in the sight of the Lord by dabbling in the idolatrous practices of Canaan. The Lord permits a foreign conqueror to come and the nation is reduced to slavery. The people repent, and cry to the Lord. He raises up a Judge to deliver the nation. Then follows the story of the Judge, drawn from ancient tradition and legend. When the Judge has done his work, "the land has rest", until it again falls into apostasy.

By the use of this framework the exploits of twelve Judges are linked together. For some of these heroes—Tola, Jair, Ibzan, and Elon—the editors had very little information beyond their names. For others, notably Gideon and Samson, they had a whole cycle of legends at their disposal. Out of the diverse material available they constructed an artificial scheme of twelve leaders, one for each of the tribes of Israel. Their aim in this process was not to tell the factual history of the age, but to illustrate by twelve concrete cases the philosophy of history spelled out in the framework of the stories.

The basic idea is simple to the point of being naïve. When Israel was obedient to the covenant she prospered. When she violated the covenant, especially by adopting idolatrous worship, she suffered defeat and oppression. Repentance brought deliverance and restoration. The book of Judges is, thus, a twelve-fold illustration, drawn from history, of the belief that prosperity and obedience go hand in hand as effect and cause.

This view of history is characteristic of the Deuteronomic

74

school of writers, and is to be found everywhere in the great history of Israel which this school produced. The Deuteronomic history includes the books of Deuteronomy, Joshua, Judges, Samuel, and Kings, telling the story of the nation from its formation in the wilderness to its end with the fall of Jerusalem in 586 B.C. The entire history is an elaboration of the thesis that obedience to the Lord is "life and good" while disobedience is "death and evil" (Deuteronomy 30: 15).

What the Deuteronomists taught cannot be put aside as a childish oversimplification of the complexity of history. Their desire to emphasize that God is concerned with and active in the affairs of nations is an authentic part of the Judeo-Christian tradition. Their insistence that faithfulness and sin are not matters of indifference is also of the first importance. Sin does bring disaster, and faithful obedience to the will of God is the source of strength and stability in the life of men, or all religion is illusion. The Deuteronomists are not dour prophets of doom. They know that the God of Israel is a God of loving kindness. He waits only for His people to repent before He comes to their aid and deliverance.

Where Deuteronomic thought failed was when it was applied to individuals in the rigid formula that suffering always comes from sin. If this is true, it follows that every sufferer is a sinner. Against this heartless doctrine the book of Job registered a vivid protest. Not every man in pain can be labeled "sinner", nor can every rich and bloated plutocrat be hailed as righteous because he is prosperous. Religious truth must be tempered with the common sense to see when it will fit the facts and when it will not.

The Covenant Community

Our brief review of the origin of Israel has made clear that the covenant entered into at Sinai between God and the people provides the basic clue to understanding the entire Old Testament. The nation came into existence as a covenant community, and everything distinctive about it arises out of the covenant.

But what is different in this from any nation looking back with reverence on its origin? The founders of Rome, Romulus and Remus, were of divine birth, and the city owed its origin to the care of the gods for their children. The Aztecs were led to their homeland by the divine Hummingbird Wizard. In more recent times the French and American Revolutions produced new nations out of historical events, which, although not interpreted as acts of God, are, nevertheless, looked to with reverence as defining and forming the nation. Yet in none of these cases has the foundation of a nation produced anything like the covenant community of Israel.

The uniqueness of Israel's history is not in the Sinai covenant itself, but in the chain of divine action which led up to the covenant. What happened at Sinai cannot, therefore, be understood apart from the saving act of God in Egypt and the interpretation given to it by Moses. Because of these events Israel regarded her existence as a gift of God, and her destiny as dependent on her faithfulness to her origin.

In Canaan she encountered new influences, and novel institutions were grafted into her constitution: prophecy, the annual festivals, the development of the priesthood, and the increasing complexity of the sacrifices. But as the nation grew each new element was brought into her life under the controlling influence of the covenant. What was borrowed had to conform to the covenant pattern, and anything which could not be so conformed was opposed.

The struggles of Israel in Canaan were, thus, only in part economic and political. They always had a deeper religious dimension. Could the new be seen as a gift of God, contributing to and enlarging the life of the nation, without encroaching on or altering its covenant structure?

The New Covenant

Having seen the origin of Israel and her first growing pains in this perspective, the reader knows that the most fundamental sections of the Old Testament are Exodus 1–15, the liberation from Egypt, and its sequel in Exodus 19: 1–23: 33, the giving of the covenant. Without these there is no Israel and no Bible.

It is possible to say "no Bible", including the New Testament, because Christianity conceived the new act of God in Jesus Christ as a deliverance, not from bondage to Pharaoh, but from slavery to sin. The act of liberation was seen as issuing in a new covenant community, the Christian Church, without the racial and geographic limitations of Israel, but as firmly bound to God by ties of gratitude and trust as was its ancient counterpart. The sacred book of Christianity is accurately described as "The New Covenant". The word "covenant" emphasizes the continuity between Israel and the Church, both communities formed by the saving power of God. The word "new" forces attention to the transformation that took place when the covenant was broken away from its national setting and became world-embracing, and when its centre was shifted from the historic event of the exodus to the living presence of Christ in His Church.

7

THE DIVINE-HUMAN ENCOUNTER

It is a long jump from the beginning of the Iron Age to the beginning of the Atomic Age. Between the two lie the whole history of Israel, the introduction of Christianity, and the long story of western civilization. In the hands of a modern reader the Bible is an ancient book. Its antiquated civilization of shepherds in the fields, and wars fought with sword and bow, seems remote from towering office buildings, lurking submarines, and air space filled with commerce and war. The customs, ideals, and even the language of the Bible leave a gulf of staggering width between its world and ours. Yet, despite the span of centuries and the wide differences in culture, the Bible has a message relevant for to-day, and the making of Israel is part of our own history.

In looking for the relevance of the Bible to our time the most common error is to seek it in the details of the stories. Disappointment and frustration are one result of this enterprise. Another is a deadly Biblical literalism, which loses the meaning of the text in blind insistence on the accuracy of its minute parts. The bitterest arguments about the Bible are usually over such factual matters, and, tragically, leave the heart of the matter untouched.

The permanent significance of the Biblical writings lies in the stance which the writers adopted towards the meaning of life. Their understanding of the nature of God and of man, and of what happens in the encounter between man and God, is relevant to every age. The Scriptures are valued and read, not for what they tell about the culture and politics of the Iron Age, but for their insight into the essential nature of the divine-human encounter.

The Rule of God

The Exodus narrative and the history of the conquest of Canaan are rich in this deeper meaning of the Scriptures. We do not face bondage to a Pharaoh, but we experience forms of slavery as real and binding as the Israelites endured in Egypt. To know that the universe is ruled by a God who characteristically acts to free the slave and to bring liberty into every situation of oppression is as important to the twentieth century as to the Israelites in Egypt. The details of Moses' life would be merely part of the curious lore of the past, if they did not also carry the message that God's way with mankind is to work through servants of His choosing, and that the full capacities of life are realized only if a man is willing to submerge his personal interests in the service of God and of the people.

Altars have long ago ceased to smoke and animals to die for the sacrifices, but the *meaning* of the sacrificial ritual retains its significance. The covenant community can be sustained only if it takes seriously its position in the presence of the holy God, and attempts to preserve its holiness. Confession of sin and trust in the redemptive power of God were the realities for which the sacrificial system stood. They are still essential elements in the religious life of the modern world. Some things are not outgrown with the passage of time. One of them is the need of weak and erring human beings for the presence, guidance, and correction of God. Altar, ark, and tabernacle symbolized these to ancient Israel, and, while the symbols are no longer valid, the realities for which they stood retain their ancient force.

The community remembrance of the saving act of God, which marked all Old Testament worship, has changed in form in the course of the centuries. No longer is the covenant renewed in an annual festival at a central shrine as it was in the days of the Judges. But the Jewish family shares the Passover meal, and the Christian Church joins in the Lord's Supper. Both these acts are memorials of the delivering power of God. In both the present community testifies to its oneness with God's people in the past, and expresses its hope for the future. The Passover ends, "Next year in Jerusalem", and the Holy Communion, "As often as ye eat this bread and drink this cup ye do show forth the Lord's death, *till he come*". Underlying the difference in form is the common conviction, shaped by a people liberated from slavery over three thousand years ago, that the present worshipping generation is a link in a chain of divine activity by which past, present, and future are bound together in the purpose of God.

God Claims the Whole of Life

Readers of Israel's legal literature are often disturbed by the apparent irrelevance of most of the laws to their own situation. If every law must be applied to modern life, the mistrust is well founded. But Israel's law is not like a traffic code, designed to serve the convenience of society. Its importance is not in its detailed commandments but in its setting in the covenant. It is a perpetual reminder that God has given this people all it possesses, and that it owes Him total obedience and service.

The scope of the law, dealing as it does with such mundane things as cattle and houses, stands as witness to the fact that the saving act of God lays its claim on the whole of life. A religion which takes the exodus faith at all seriously can never confine itself to a spiritual side of man's nature, leaving the rest of his personality to be run by the laws of economics and politics. The law insists that every act is a religious act, and that man is judged as much by how he runs the office as by how he says his prayers.

The true successors of the Biblical faith, then, are not those who have memorized long sections of the Scriptures, or who profess to believe "every word of the Bible", but those who adopt the same posture towards life as that which inspired ancient Israel.

Materialist and Religious

In the contemporary world there are two competing views of life, which may be called the materialist and the religious view.

The first of these judges all things by what can be seen, measured and controlled. The only realities are those subject to human observation. History is the record of the progress of mankind, with occasional and temporary setbacks, in controlling his environment, and refining his mental processes and artistic sensitivity. The ideal society is one in control of its environment, adjusted to the forces playing upon it, and living in prosperity, security, and peace. The individual works to make a satisfactory adjustment to the social and economic world in which he lives.

There are, of course, many levels on which the materialist view of life manifests itself. At one extreme it produces a static existence, without direction or goal. To keep the human machine going for its full life span, with a minimum of pain and with some interludes for fun, is the only detectable purpose in many modern communities. The frenzied activity of modern life has with some justice been attributed to fear that stopping for a moment would expose the meaninglessness of the activity and lead to despair.

At the opposite extreme is materialism raised to the rank of philosophy and social theory. The laws of economics dictate the course of history, and the great revolution of the proletariat will eventually produce a classless society of perfect equality and justice. Purpose is, thus, generated out of the material of history itself. Messiahs are produced who announce the dawn of the new age, and zealots devote themselves with singleness of purpose and vigorous self-discipline to its realization. Between the extremes of Communism and hedonism (belief in pleasure as the chief good) all intermediate shades of opinion and practice exist, united by the common assumption that the material and the human hold all the significance that there is to life.

The religious view believes that the meaning of life is not

conferred by anything within history or nature, but is given from beyond the realms of time and matter by God, the Creator. The fundamental adjustment of life is not to the environment but to God. On this view man is incapable of understanding himself or of directing his steps, except as God reveals to him the purpose and significance of his existence. Within the scope of the world religions this view takes many forms, but the most thorough statement of what it is and what it implies is given in the exodus faith of Israel. No arguments are advanced for the existence of God. But the covenant relationship between God and the nation is seen as that which gives it purpose and movement, lifting it from nonentity to nationhood.

Christianity is not the Servant of Culture

Popular Christianity of the twentieth century is plagued by a sorry confusion of the two views of life, for which the Churches must assume some responsibility. Christianity is too often represented as a convenient way of adjusting to the social and economic environment. "Families that pray together stay together" and those who practice "the Christian virtues" keep their jobs or get better ones. In this way Christianity becomes the servant of culture. It is made to serve the goals set by society, and is valued for what the people can get out of it. Christianity is "sold" to the community on the ground of its utility, as if it were the spiritual arm of scientific technology.

In the exodus narratives the point is hammered home at Sinai, at the Sea of Reeds, and in the wilderness that man does not exist to be served by God, but to serve Him. He is not called to extract a profit from his faith, but to give himself in the service of God. Even the practitioners of the Holy War recognized that they were asked to jeopardize their lives in complete trust in the God who could give or withhold the victory. Their more pacifist and cultured successors often wish to determine the strategy and tactics of their own lives, and expect God to come in as an ally on their terms.

The bitter struggles in Canaan between the Lord and Baal indicate that between religion based on the sovereignty of God, and culture derived from the attempt of man to assert his supremacy, there is a permanent tension. It can only be resolved by bending culture to the service of God; never, without disaster, by reducing the deity to a servant of culture.

The difficulties created by the tension between religion and culture are nowhere clearer than in the mission field. Should a convert be turned away because he refuses to bury his dead in violation of his own tradition that the body should be consumed by fire? Ought a convert be asked to divorce two of his three wives? How much of the pagan life may be permitted to continue within the Church? Israel faced similar problems in Canaan, and so in subtler form does the citizen of the "Christian" democracy. No solution can be given that will cover all cases at once, but the Biblical narrative is clear on how the problem should be handled. The central core of the faith must be carefully defined, as Israel did in her covenant. Only what can be conformed to this core may be adopted. The rest may be tolerated, if it is neutral to the faith, but, if it contradicts the central core, it must be opposed and excluded.

It should be observed that these high ideals were not always maintained in Israel. The chosen People had all the weaknesses which we possess. The warrior in the Holy War often fought for land and gain. The people murmured in the wilderness, when they were not fed. Gideon's father built the altar to Baal in order to be on the safe side in ensuring the success of his farming. One of the real glories of the Old Testament is the honesty with which it shows both sides of the coin. We could hardly see ourselves in a people whole-heartedly devoted to the highest in its religion, but we can with profit identify ourselves with a nation torn between devotion and self-gratification.

Israel's Faith Pioneered the Gospel

The Biblical account of the origin of Israel makes it clear that the most important question faced by the religious view of life is that of the nature and activity of God. The documents we have studied pioneered ideas concerning God which continued throughout the history of Israel, were taken up in Christianity, and are central to the life and thought of the contemporary Church.

The New Testament is dominated by the idea of the love of God. "God so loved the world that he gave his only Son, that whoever believes in him should not perish but have eternal life" (John 3 : 16). This inspired summary of the gospel has its roots firmly planted in the exodus tradition. The same is true of St. Paul's teaching that salvation is a gift offered to the Christian by the love of God poured out in Jesus Christ (the concept of grace).

These New Testament writers assumed that their readers were familiar with the fundamentals of Israel's exodus faith, and, hence, took little pains to guard against the misuse of the idea of the love of God. If, however, this Old Testament rootage is forgotten, it can easily degenerate into nothing more than a sentimental attachment of God to the human race, by which He is loosely tolerant of sin, and vaguely well-disposed to mankind.

The grace of God, revealed in Israel's history, was not a sentiment or an emotion, but a kind of action. It was liberation directed towards the needy and the oppressed. It broke the tyrant and set the people free. After the deliverance it took the form of guidance in the wilderness, sustenance through the difficulties of the journey, and the gift of the land. None of this was earned by Israel. It was all given by her God. Even when the rebellious spirit of the nation brought disaster, this too was the grace of God summoning the people to repentance and restoration.

The love of God in the New Testament has all of these qualities. It is, first of all, the freedom-conferring act of God in history through Jesus Christ. Like the grace of God in the exodus it operates in salvation, guidance, sustenance, chastisement, and forgiveness. It is not directed to one nation, but towards mankind, and it is revealed, not on the mountain, but on the Cross. The magnitude of these differences should not be underestimated, but, by the same token, the difference should not be seen as complete. With the Sinai covenant a new way of understanding God was born. During the centuries God nurtured the spark in Israel, until in due time it burst into flame in Jesus Christ. The chief relevance of the exodus is that it taught men to think soberly of the grace of God.

Man's Unfulfilment

Second in importance only to the activity of God is the problem of the nature of man. What is it to be human? The origin of Israel sheds light on this also, for at no point in her history was Israel capable of meeting her own needs. She could not fight free of Egypt, or guide herself in the wilderness, or battle her way into the promised land. Her record is one of dependence on God. The only thing she possessed in her own right was the ability to assert her independence, and to say to God in effect, "I have no need of thee".

Applied to human nature in general Israel's self-understanding means that man is incapable of fulfilling any of the deepest longings, hopes, and aspirations of his own nature. Yet in radical freedom he is able to deny his creaturehood, and attempt to live off his own resources. The assertion of independence is a high road to disaster, and the only salvation is for man to swallow his pride and accept the salvation of God as a gift.

This understanding of human nature is particularly hard for modern man to accept. In an age of unequalled technical progress, man has come to think of himself as an invincible conqueror. He talks of the conquest of the sea, of the air, and now of space. In such an atmosphere of self-sufficiency a religion which teaches the helplessness and inadequacy of man is certain to encounter hard travelling.

In spite of the difficulties under which it is placed in a self-confident age, Christianity cannot give up its belief in the dependent nature of man without destroying itself. If science, education, or philosophy can save mankind, God's action in so radical a form as the Cross is a superfluity, and the whole tradition from Sinai to Calvary is an immense error. The evidences of recent history, however, lend support to the Biblical view. The emancipation of man from the "tyranny of religion" has been marked by two world wars in which refinements of barbarism were practiced at which savages would have shuddered. The age of man's greatest achievement has become the age of anxiety.

The ideal relationship between Israel and God is trust. As the stories of Israel's infancy portray it, trust involves two elements; acknowledgment of the sovereignty of God and of His absolute right to rule over the affairs of the nation, and commitment of all the talents of individuals and community in obedience to the divine lordship. This relationship found its way into New Testament thought, where, enriched and enlarged, it is called "faith".

It would be difficult to estimate the influence on human history of St. Paul's formulation of the gospel as "grace working through faith". Yet both the concepts in St. Paul's statement had their origin in the covenant religion of Israel .

Man's Reflection of God

The laws of the covenant have not infrequently been put forward as guides to practical living. In their detail, however, most of the laws are inappropriate to or irrelevant to modern life. The spirit, not the letter, is the important thing. Within the covenant obedience to the law is response to the saving act of God. The response takes two forms. On the one hand it is humility and a due sense of one's own unworthiness. On the other it involves an imitation of the qualities ascribed to God. The latter aspect of